SUPERVISING EMPLOYEES WITH DISABILITIES
Beyond ADA Compliance

Mary B. Dickson

A FIFTY-MINUTE™ SERIES BOOK

CRISP PUBLICATIONS, INC.
Menlo Park, California

SUPERVISING EMPLOYEES WITH DISABILITIES
Beyond ADA Compliance

Mary B. Dickson

CREDITS:
Editor: **Brenda Machosky**
Designer: **Carol Harris**
Typesetting: **ExecuStaff**
Cover Design: **Carol Harris**
Cover Artwork: **Priscilla Hagan**
Artwork: **Ralph Mapson**

Printed in the United States of America by Bawden Printing Company.

English language Crisp books are distributed worldwide. Our major international distributors include:

CANADA: Reid Publishing, Ltd., Box 69559—109 Thomas St., Oakville, Ontario Canada L6J 7R4. TEL: (416) 842-4428; FAX: (416) 842-9327

AUSTRALIA: Career Builders, P.O. Box 1051, Springwood, Brisbane, Queensland, Australia 4127. TEL: 841-1061, FAX: 841-1580

NEW ZEALAND: Career Builders, P.O. Box 571, Manurewa, Auckland, New Zealand. TEL: 266-5276, FAX: 266-4152

JAPAN: Phoenix Associates Co., Mizuho Bldg. 2-12-2, Kami Osaki, Shinagawa-Ku, Tokyo 141, Japan. TEL: 3-443-7231, FAX: 3-443-7640

Selected Crisp titles are also available in other languages. Contact International Rights Manager Tim Polk at (800) 442-7477 for more information.

Library of Congress Catalog Card Number 92-75714
Dickson, Mary B.
Supervising Employees with Disabilities
ISBN 1-56052-209-7

This book is printed on recyclable paper with soy ink.

PREFACE

The Americans with Disabilities Act of 1990 (ADA) has created new opportunities for America's 43 million people with disabilities. Unfortunately, as with any new social movement or law, it has also created fear and misunderstanding among people without disabilities, or, as some people call them, CRABs (**C**urrently **R**egarded as **A**ble **B**odied).

As a supervisor, you have a choice about how you view the ADA.

- You can join the doomsayers who say it will result in huge lawsuits, put them out of business, or require extraordinary effort to supervise a new group of people.

  OR

- You can look at it as an opportunity to contribute to your organization's profitability *and* to give qualified, talented, capable people with disabilities the dignity and financial benefits of a job that appropriately uses their skills. You can use it as a way to give people their fair chance at the American Dream!

The goal of this book is to help you examine your job as a supervisor in relation to the ADA and how it relates to all of your employees, CRABs as well as people with disabilities.

Mary B. Dickson

The information in this book is designed to be general and timely information on the Americans with Disabilities Act of 1990 (ADA). The author is not an attorney, and she is not rendering legal advice to the reader or assistance with individual employer action. Every employment situation is different. Readers should consult the person with the disability first, then appropriate agencies or competent legal counsel regarding how these matters relate to their business or personal affairs.

ABOUT THIS BOOK

Supervising Employees with Disabilities is not like most books. It has a unique "self-paced" format that encourages a reader to become personally involved. Designed to be "read with a pencil," there are an abundance of exercises, activities, assessments and cases that invite participation.

The objective of this book is to specifically address the daily concerns of supervisors who work with employees with disabilities. As you work through the book, you will recognize that supervising employees with disabilities is not significantly different from supervising other employees. (General knowledge of the ADA will be helpful for this book does not explain or interpret the law.)

Supervising Employees with Disabilities (and the other self-improvement books listed in the back of this book) can be used effectively in a number of ways. Here are some possibilities:

Individual Study. Because the book is self-instructional, all that is needed is a quiet place, some time and a pencil. Completing the activities and exercises should provide not only valuable feedback, but also practical ideas about measuring and improving customer satisfaction.

Workshops and Seminars. The book is ideal for preassigned reading prior to a workshop or seminar. With the basics in hand, the quality of participation should improve. More time can be spent on concept extensions and applications during the program. The book is also effective when distributed at the beginning of a session.

Remote Location Training. Copies can be sent to those not able to attend "home office" training sessions.

Informal Study Groups. Thanks to the format, brevity and low cost, this book is ideal for "brown-bag" or other informal group sessions.

There are other possibilities that depend on the objectives of the user. One thing is for sure, even after it has been read, this book will serve as excellent reference material which can be easily reviewed. Good luck!

ABOUT THE AUTHOR

Mary B. Dickson is president of Creative Compliance Management, a consulting firm that specializes in assisting organizations to maximize their human resources. She helps them to implement the Americans with Disabilities Act confidently and cost-effectively. She provides training and consultation in ADA policy development, job analysis and job descriptions, and performs accessibility studies. She helps supervisors and colleagues become sensitive to co-workers and customers with disabilities. In addition, she conducts training on a variety of management and supervisory development topics.

Ms. Dickson serves as a technical consultant to media firms developing ADA training materials and is co-author of *The Americans with Disabilities Act: Impact on Training* and *The Americans with Disabilities Act: Techniques for Accommodation* published by the American Society for Training and Development (ASTD) in 1992. She is National Director of ASTD's Disabilities Awareness Network.

Ms. Dickson has a master's degree in vocational rehabilitation. She is a former Director of Rehabilitation Services for the Oregon Commission for the Blind and taught at the Center for Continuing Education in Rehabilitation at Seattle University. She has hired and supervised people with disabilities.

Ms. Dickson welcomes your comments and questions. She also welcomes the opportunity to talk with you about how her training and consulting services could benefit your organization. You may reach her at:

Creative Compliance Management
13629 SE Grant Court
Portland, OR 97233
(503) 255-9318 (503) 255-7408 (fax)

ACKNOWLEDGMENTS

A number of people contributed ideas, technical expertise, and feedback during the writing and editing process. Special thanks go to:

Gail Benson of Southern New England Telecommunications Corporation, New Haven, CT
Carolyn Thompson of CBT Training Systems, Frankfort, IL
Gary Jenks, Paul Short, Sue Thompson, and Jay Harris of SEH America, Inc., Vancouver, WA
Ken Cross, Human Resource Specialties, Inc., Lake Oswego, OR

For a legal review, I gratefully acknowledge Eileen Drake of Stoel Rives Boley Jones & Grey, Portland, OR.

As a role model, Arty Frost is unsurpassed.

Special love and thanks to Blaine Dickson for a quarter century of love and support.

Dedication

This book is dedicated to

- the many people with disabilities whose skills and commitment make believers out of nonbelievers, and
- supervisors who believe enough in themselves and in qualified people with disabilities to make a significant contribution to the workplace.

ABOUT THE COVER ARTIST

The cover artwork is courtesy of Priscilla Hagan, a weaver who is also a vocational rehabilitation counselor for the Oregon Vocational Rehabilitation Division and a person with multiple sclerosis. Her weaving, 24″ × 32″, is interwoven inlay strips of varied wools including boucles and tweeds on a linen ground with shots of copper metallic.

The interwoven structure represents to this book's author the interweaving of people of all ''textures'' in the workplace, those with different ethnic backgrounds, genders, and physical and mental abilities. All people, woven together with a common goal, contribute to the whole, the fabric of our workplace.

CONTENTS

CONTENTS (continued)

INTRODUCTION

The Americans with Disabilities Act of 1990 (ADA) offers organizations opportunities to include qualified people with disabilities in their workforce in new and exciting ways. If you are like many people, you are updating your knowledge of people with disabilities in order to make the ADA work effectively in your organization.

Many of us grew up with negative cultural programming that told us not to stare at anyone who is ''different,'' and not to expect people with disabilities to work alongside us in industry.

With the ADA now changing the way we do business, we need to put aside our cultural programming and accept people with disabilities in our workplace.

This book will help you recognize that:

► We can communicate effectively with people regardless of physical or mental disabilities.

► We can help nondisabled colleagues of people with disabilities to accept and get along with disabled co-workers while maintaining confidentiality about physical and mental conditions.

► We can obey the ADA and maintain productivity and harmonious working relationships.

As a supervisor, you are faced with an aging workforce. Many current employees, long valued for their contributions to your company's bottom line, face the potential of a disabling condition, from repetitive motion syndrome to cancer to loss of vision or hearing. How will you supervise them should they become disabled? Will their disability make any difference in their productivity or the way you and their co-workers relate to them?

Your attitude is a key factor. Your communication skills, willingness to deal with change and creativity are all skills which make you successful as a supervisor. This book should help you recognize that these skills and attitudes will make you more effective supervising *all* employees.

INTRODUCTION (continued)

Developing Your Supervisory Philosophy about the ADA

When you become a supervisor, you develop a philosophy for your new role, either consciously or unconsciously. You will also want to develop a philosophy of how you will comply with the ADA and supervise qualified people with disabilities.

Let's look at three possible ADA supervisory philosophies. Consider where you presently fit, then monitor your attitude as you work through this book.

Tom or Tammy Traditional. As supervisors, Tom and Tammy . . .

✓ May regard the ADA as just another law and will do the minimum necessary to ensure compliance.

✓ May never have had any contact with people with disabilities and think that they should stay home or in an institution or work in sheltered workshops, if at all.

✓ May be concerned that hiring a person with a disability would cause problems with co-worker acceptance, lowered productivity, and poor quality.

Maria and Mark Middle-of-the-Road. As supervisors, they . . .

✓ May be aware of the ADA and its general provisions but do not worry about the details.

✓ May think people with disabilities who work are ''amazing'' and ''courageous,'' but cannot imagine having someone with a disability working in their department.

✓ Would probably only hire a person with a disability hesitantly, and if that person did not work out, would not hire another one.

Ann and Andy Assertive. As supervisors, Ann and Andy . . .

✓ Look at new initiatives, laws, and regulations as somewhat of a bother to learn about, but once they understand them, they will wholeheartedly comply.

✓ May aggressively seek ways in which the laws can benefit them and their department.

✓ May have had classmates in school with disabilities and feel comfortable interacting with them.

✓ May look at the ADA and say, ''Hmm, how can this help me meet my department's goals? How can I make my department a leader in this area?''

✓ May look for opportunities to establish links with schools and organizations that help find employment for qualified people with disabilities and offer employment to someone with potential.

Where do you fit in this list of characteristics? Are you closer to a Tom or Tammy than an Ann or Andy, or do you fit someplace in the middle? Keep in mind that how you deal with change may impact the way you deal with the ADA. Throughout this book, we will look at how these supervisors react to the ADA. Follow the scenarios with them to help you develop your own ADA philosophy.

Before you begin to work through this book, take the True/False test on the next three pages to check your understanding of The Americans with Disabilities Act. (See Appendix pages 119-122 for the answers.)

The Americans with Disabilities Act of 1990 (ADA)

TRUE OR FALSE QUIZ

The Americans With Disabilities Act is designed to remove employment barriers for qualified individuals with disabilities. The ADA requires employers to identify what reasonable accommodations might be necessary to allow an employee to perform the essential functions of a specific job. The following quiz will help determine the training needs of your organization to address full and equal employment opportunities for all individuals under this new law. **Circle the correct answer.**

True **False** **1.** The Americans With Disabilities Act protects all qualified individuals with disabilities regardless of their citizenship status or nationality.

True **False** **2.** An individual with a disability may choose to file a legal claim under a state discrimination law.

True **False** **3.** When symptoms of a disability are controlled by medication, an individual is no longer considered disabled.

True **False** **4.** Individuals who were economically disadvantaged as children qualify as disabled.

True **False** **5.** Obesity is not generally considered a disabling impairment.

True **False** **6.** The presence of a physical impairment is sufficient evidence of a disability.

True **False** **7.** Acceptance of an individual with a disability by co-workers or customers is important to the hiring process.

True **False** **8.** An employer may consider the applicant's future health when making an employment decision.

True **False** **9.** The essential function of a job may be directly related to the size of the staff.

True **False** **10.** Job descriptions are required by the Americans With Disabilities Act.

True **False** 11. A job applicant with chronic breathing problems requiring frequent rest periods that affect productivity would be protected by the ADA.

True **False** 12. Employers must modify the job application process to enable qualified applicants with disabilities equal opportunities.

True **False** 13. Employers may offer a health insurance policy that excludes coverage for pre-existing conditions.

True **False** 14. If a current employee is unable to perform a job with a reasonable accommodation, he must be considered for reassignment to another available position.

True **False** 15. An employee may be required to eat lunch at his desk if the company cafeteria is inaccessible.

True **False** 16. If accessible public transportation delays the arrival of an employee by fifteen minutes, his chronic tardiness is grounds for dismissal.

True **False** 17. Cost may be a reason for not making an accommodation.

True **False** 18. Employers may exclude a job applicant who poses a direct risk to the safety of others.

True **False** 19. Drug testing is prohibited by the Americans With Disabilities Act.

True **False** 20. A non-disabled job applicant who shares a home with an AIDS patient is not a good candidate because he may experience frequent absences.

True **False** 21. When several effective accommodations are available, the employer must comply with the employee's preference.

True **False** 22. Employers may be found liable for not addressing reasonable accommodations for an employee who has kept his disability a secret.

TRUE OR FALSE QUIZ (continued)

True **False** **23.** When a reasonable accommodation allows a job applicant with a disability to perform a job, he must be given preference over other candidates.

True **False** **24.** If a necessary accommodation is refused, the employee may no longer be considered qualified.

True **False** **25.** When it is obvious that a job applicant is disabled (Example: uses a wheelchair), ADA encourages inquiries about the nature of the disability.

True **False** **26.** Dexterity tests may be given at anytime during the job application process.

True **False** **27.** A job offer may be conditioned on the results of a medical examination.

True **False** **28.** Medical information should be routinely updated and kept in the employee's personnel file.

True **False** **29.** An employee could pay for providing a reasonable accommodation if it was found to be an undue hardship for the employer.

True **False** **30.** The Americans With Disabilities Act encourages alternative solutions to resolve disputes prior to legal action.

P A R T

I

The Positive Employment Picture

PEOPLE WITH DISABILITIES

A Well-Kept Human Resource Secret

As a supervisor, you hire people who can help your organization make money or provide good service. You have undoubtedly noticed that the workplace is changing, and you have a different pool of applicants than you have had in the past.

That pool now includes qualified people with disabilities. Although many people think that the Americans with Disabilities Act is responsible for introducing this new element of the workforce, many companies discovered long before the ADA that employees who were disabled were productive workers. The March–April 1992 issue of *In the Mainstream* reviews 11 studies related to the employment of persons with disabilities.

Results are consistent among all studies from 1948 to 1990:

- Work performance: good to excellent
- Insurance costs: no increase
- Turnover: lower than workers without disabilities
- Absenteeism: lower than coworkers without disabilities
- Accident rates: lower than other employees
- Accommodations: perceived by companies as not prohibitively costly

The Survey Highlights of a 1991 Harris Poll reveal that "more than 4 out of 5 Americans believe that disabled workers are equally or more productive than average workers. However, only just over half of those with a regular job rate their employers' policies for the employment of disabled people positively" (p. viii).

Some people worry about how co-workers would feel about having their work hours or job duties changed to accommodate a new worker with a disability. A study done by the Bureau of National Affairs in early 1992 found that over half would think it was fair, another quarter might not think it was fair but would not protest, and only 16 percent would protest. That number will probably decrease as people have positive experiences with disabled colleagues.

A WELL-KEPT HUMAN RESOURCE SECRET (continued)

Companies that have enjoyed notable successes include:

✓ Marriott Corporation has hired over 8,000 people with disabilities and has found a lower turnover rate than among their nondisabled employees.

✓ Pizza Hut has calculated that it has saved over $2.2 million in turnover costs.

✓ Little Tikes Company, of Hudson, Ohio, hired 15 hearing impaired workers and provided accommodations such as flashing lights on forklifts, an interpreter for the monthly staff meeting, and sign language classes for hearing employees. They also created transitional jobs to return injured workers back to work. They have realized a high retention rate and impressive levels of dedication and commitment to the company.

✓ The University of Massachusetts Medical Center has hired nearly 400 employees with disabilities and one assistant (who is also disabled). Accommodations cost *less than $700 annually.*

✓ SEH America, Inc., in Vancouver, Washington, has a successful supported employment program that employs workers with developmental disabilities.

✓ National companies that have recognized the skills of employees with disabilities include Honeywell, IBM, Apple, and the Bell System.

It is not only large, well-known companies that have found capable employees with disabilities making a difference. Companies of all sizes, in small towns as well as large cities, benefit from hiring good employees!

- John Zandy, a partner in a Connecticut law firm, says of employing an intern with a disability, ''I gave him difficult assignments, and he returned high-quality legal work. We simply gave someone with a good mind an opportunity to excel.''

- Kreonite, Inc., manufacturer of photographic and graphic arts film based in Wichita, Kansas, has dropped its turnover rate from 32 percent to 10 to 12 percent by hiring persons with disabilities.

In addition to organizational benefits, individuals benefit from contact with qualified people with disabilities. One supervisor said, ''As a result of our experience with a developmentally disabled employee, the 40 people in this department no longer frown on things like Special Olympics. Their fears of people with disabilities are gone. They are more warm-hearted and look at other people with disabilities face to face. This experience has changed us all forever.''

Talented, competent people with disabilities can make a positive difference in the workplace.

MATCH GAME EXERCISE

Match up the following well-known people in column 1 and their disability in column 2. Then think about the contribution each has made through his or her work. Compare your answers with those listed in the Appendix on page 118.

CONTRIBUTOR	DISABILITY
Cher	Head injury
Chris Burke	Polio
Bruce Jenner	Blind
James Brady	Learning disability
Stephen Hawking	Orthopedic impairment
Ray Charles	Visual impairment
Ann Jillian	Polio
Whoopi Goldberg	Learning disability
Senator Robert Dole	Epilepsy
Itzhak Perlman	Mental illness
Marlee Matlin	Deaf
President John F. Kennedy	Back problems
Mary Tyler Moore	Dyslexia
Danny Glover	Down's syndrome
Sammy Davis, Jr.	Multiple sclerosis
Annette Funicello	Amyotrophic lateral sclerosis
Governor George Wallace	Diabetes
President Franklin Roosevelt	Multiple sclerosis
Margaux Hemingway	Epilepsy
Virginia Woolf	Cancer
Representative Barbara Jordan	Paraplegia

Your organization has probably already joined this list of stars. Who in your company has made a contribution while living and working with a disability?

____

____

Not all people with disabilities are famous. Thousands live normal and productive lives without ever being in the spotlight. However, you can see from this list that people with disabilities can achieve greatness. If you see a person who uses a wheelchair and wonder how he or she could possibly do the job, just remember the president who served this country longer than any other holder of that office.

Attitude Checkpoint

How does supervisory philosophy impact an organization's success?

Tom Traditional might respond, "Well, these are big companies that can afford to have some people around who don't pull their weight."

Maria Middle-of-the-Road might say, "I think it's wonderful that those companies have hired those poor, courageous people."

Ann Assertive might ponder, "I wonder how these companies got started. It sounds like having people with disabilities around may be worth looking into."

You say, ____

____

____

____

____

____

PART

II

Disabilities: Our Attitudes and ADA Definitions

THE ORIGIN OF ATTITUDES

Each of us was raised differently; however, we may have heard some or all of the following during the years our attitudes were formed. Notice how society is changing in its attitudes.

- Many parents said to their children, "Don't stare at people with disabilities; it's not polite." Our natural curiosity and potential acceptance of people with disabilities was discouraged. We were probably not encouraged to make friends with classmates with disabilities, or invite them to lunch or to our house. This may have been similar to what we learned about people whose skin color or religion was different from ours.

  Our limited interactions and parental stereotyping are partial reasons for the difficulty in integrating people of difference into our workplace. We are now learning to react differently through emphasis on "diversity" issues.

- Movies we saw long ago showed people with disabilities as someone to pity, like Tiny Tim in *A Christmas Carol,* or as someone special, superhuman, or amazing, like Helen Keller. Today's TV shows offer a chance to see competent people with disabilities working and interacting quite differently; for example, Benny in "L.A. Law," Corky in "Life Goes On," and Tess in "Reasonable Doubts."

- Our schools once put children with disabilities in "Special Education" classes, depriving us of opportunities to learn to interact with people with disabilities as youngsters. Now, children with disabilities are "mainstreamed" as much as possible.

- We were told to be good or we would end up like people with disabilities. We were made to feel afraid of anyone who was "different." Today, we are more likely to recognize that people with disabilities are not evil or being punished for something they have done.

- We learned to equate disability with sickness. These days, we watch wheelchair athletes and participants in Special Olympics use their bodies to achive athletic feats.

- We learned that we should be nice to people with disabilities, to feel sorry for them, and not to expect much from them, and *this* attitude may not have changed much!

We may carry around the myths and stereotypes we learned from the way our culture taught us. Society is now changing; however . . .

> As a result of what we learned early in life, we may not expect people with disabilities to be productive workers or lead happy lives!

WHAT WE LEARNED AS KIDS

Before we look at what our culture has taught us about people with disabilities, take a moment to look at what *you* learned.

First Contact with a Person with a Disability

Check below those people with disabilities with whom you have had personal contact at various stages in your life. Put a "✓" in the square indicating the first person with a disability you remember.

	Name of Person					
When	**Parent**	**Sibling**	**Spouse**	**Family**	**Neighbor**	**Stranger**
Preschool						
Grade School						
High School						
College						
Work						

After you have completed this chart, notice at what point in your life most of your contacts came. Were you very young, or was your first experience later in life? The significance of this will become clear later on.

Initial Impressions of People with Disabilities

Let's look a little more in depth at the impact these people had on your life.

1. When my parents or teachers told me about people with disabilities, they said:

   ____

   ____

   ____

2. The first person with a disability I knew was: ______________________

   ____

   ____

3. When I was near the person, I felt: ______________________________

   ____

   ____

4. When I was in school, I had the following experiences with classmates or a teacher with disabilities: ______________________________

   ____

   ____

5. Since I've been in the workplace, my experiences with people with disabilities have been: ______________________________

   ____

   ____

POSSIBLE LIFE EXPERIENCES

We may have had family members or friends with disabilities. Their experiences (and ours) depended on our family situation, economics, religion, and a number of other factors.

- ► Our mother lost her vision because of diabetes and had to give up her profession.
- ► Our sister with developmental disabilities was raised in a state institution and works in a sheltered workshop.
- ► Our grandfather, who had polio as a child, had doors slammed in his face because during his working years, people who limped were excluded from the workforce.

How might your life experiences influence you as a supervisor? ____________

____

____

____

____

Our experiences may have been more positive.

- ► Our mother who was blind was able to continue her career successfully with the help of specialized equipment.
- ► Our sister who is developmentally disabled may be working and living on her own.
- ► Our grandfather may have been a successful advertising executive.

How might these experiences influence you as a supervisor? ____________

____

____

____

____

We may be open to hiring and supervising qualified individuals with disabilities because of these early, positive experiences.

There's another possibility. You may know or have known a person with a disability who was "exceptional" in some way. Perhaps a blind friend was a wonderful musician, or a person who used a wheelchair was an outstanding athlete. Maybe you saw TV coverage of the young man who uses one artificial leg and completed the Bicycle Race Across America.

From these experiences, there is a danger of generalizing that all people with disabilities are musical or athletic or have some other "super" powers. You may think that they are "amazing," "wonderful," "inspiring" or "incredible."

These become the new stereotypes and myths that may give us unrealistically high expectations. The old myths and stereotypes limit people with disabilities; the new myths and stereotypes may set people up to be more than human. We need to accept people with disabilities as *people,* with the entire range of abilities and disabilities which that includes.

You may feel better now that you know where some of your attitudes originated. They become the "backpack" we carry into the workplace. The attitudes in your backpack may mean that you struggle with the idea of having qualified people with disabilities in the workplace.

These attitudes conflict with what we must do under the ADA. The law says we must consider people with disabilities as competent, productive members of the workforce. We may need to make reasonable accommodations, but we do not have to accept lower quality or quantity from employees who have disabilities.

WORKPLACE ATTITUDES

Some of us struggle with the requirements of the ADA and with the idea of having qualified people with disabilities in their workplace. We don't expect to see people with disabilities in our workplace, so we might be hesitant to hire them; and if they were there, we would not expect high quality work from them. If, by some chance, they appeared in our organization, we would expect to be nice to them, take care of them and think they are wonderful and courageous to even try to work.

These may seem like mixed messages, and they *are* until we deal with them!

SUPERVISORS' ATTITUDES

As a supervisor, how do you deal with the influences that have shaped your attitude about people with disabilities?

Supervisors' Concerns Checklist

Check any of the concerns you have about a person with a disability reporting to you.

☐ People with disabilities don't *really* want to work.

☐ I don't know how to talk to a person with a disability.

☐ My staff would not want to work with a person with a disability.

☐ I do not know how to supervise someone with a disability.

☐ My department budget does not allow for paying for reasonable accommodations for an employee with a disability.

☐ If an employee with a disability did not work out, I could not fire the person.

☐ Other ______________________________

STOP

Stop! Do not go on until you've thought about this and answered the following question!

Three things I've learned from this exercise about my attitudes are:

1. ______________________________

2. ______________________________

3. ______________________________

SUPERVISORS' ATTITUDES (continued)

Recognize your own reaction to people with disabilities by reviewing your answers to the earlier quizzes. Admit and deal with your own reactions, and if they are negative, find a way to consciously work through them.

To gain information:

- Contact local agencies which train and place people with disabilities in jobs.
- Talk with other employers who have successfully hired employees with disabilities.
- Find other supervisors in your own organization who have supervised employees with disabilities.
- Talk with people with disabilities about their employment experiences.
- Expose yourself to people who have had positive experiences.
- Look for and celebrate successful experiences with people with disabilities, both in your personal life and on the job.

What else can you do to repack your backpack? ______________________

____

____

We've been concentrating on how these messages impact you as the supervisor. (Now you need to realize that the same influences impact those whom you supervise.)

CO-WORKERS' ATTITUDES

You can help the members of your work group lighten their backpacks by becoming a role model. You can take steps such as these to deal with your employees' misperceptions, myths and stereotypes.

- You might want to talk with those you supervise, either individually or in small, informal groups, to understand their perceptions. Maybe they have no qualms about having co-workers with disabilities. Perhaps they have had positive personal or professional experiences that have led them to accept people with disabilities.

- Look at introducing qualified people with disabilities in your workplace as another aspect of diversifying the workplace. If your organization offers training on diversity, talk with the training director to ensure that disabilities are covered in the training. Request that such training deal not only with laws, but also with awareness, sensitivity, and communication skills. This will help employees feel more comfortable in dealing with people who are different from those with whom they are accustomed to working.

- Include a video on disability awareness and sensitivity in staff meetings, or ask someone from a community agency that provides services to people with a specific disability such as epilepsy to come to a staff meeting so you can all learn accurate information about that condition.

- Invite people with various disabilities to speak informally to help employees update their knowledge and attitudes.

- You can distribute pamphlets about rehabilitation agencies, and invite speakers to briefly describe their services, which may include job analysis, technical assistance in determining reasonable accommodations, and referrals of appropriately trained workers.

Probably the best way for employees to update their attitudes about people with disabilities is to successfully work alongside a disabled colleague. When a qualified person is hired, appropriate accommodations are made, an atmosphere of acceptance is created in the workplace, and supervisors increase chances for success. The supervisor's attitude has a direct bearing on the success of all employees, and a willingness to give a qualified person with a disability the chance to be successful sets the tone for the rest of the workgroup.

Attitude Checkpoint

How might our three supervisors react to employees with disabilities in their workplace?

Tammy Traditional might say, "Oh, I remember this guy with one leg. My mother always told me not to stare at him, and to stay away from him because he was different."

Mark Middle-of-the-Road might say, "There was a blind guy who went to my school. I was always amazed he could find his way to the cafeteria and eat like the rest of us."

Andy Assertive might say, "I have a friend who has epilepsy. Once people stopped being afraid of him, he got a good job as a computer systems analyst."

You say, ____

____

____

____

____

____

THE ADA DEFINITION OF DISABILITY

According to the *Technical Assistance Manual of the ADA,* an ''individual with a disability'' is someone who . . .

- Has a ***physical*** or ***mental impairment*** that ***substantially limits*** one or more ***major life activities,***
- Has a ***record of such an impairment,*** or
- Is ***regarded as having such an impairment.***

Persons who have a known association or relationship with an individual with a disability are also protected from discrimination.

ADA Key Phrases

Let's take a closer look at the key phrases in this definition more closely.

Physical Impairment

Physical impairment is defined by the ADA as ''any physiological disorder, or condition, cosmetic disfigurement, or anatomical loss affecting one or more of the following body systems: neurological, musculoskeletal, special sense organs, respiratory (including speech organs), cardiovascular, reproductive, digestive, genito-urinary, hemic and lymphatic, skin, and endocrine.''

Mental Impairment

Mental impairment is defined as ''any mental or psychological disorder, such as mental retardation, organic brain syndrome, emotional or mental illness, and specific learning disabilities.''

There is no comprehensive list of all impairments, since they can occur singly or in combination. An impairment is determined without regard to medications or assistive devices that a person may use. For example, a person may use an artifical leg but may still be considered disabled.

Contagious diseases are considered impairments, although an employer does not have to hire or retain anyone whose contagious disease poses a direct threat to health or safety if no reasonable accommodation could reduce or eliminate the threat.

ADA KEY PHRASES (continued)

Substantially Limits

Substantially limits means that ''an individual must be unable to perform, or be significantly limited in the ability to perform, an activity compared to an average person in the general population.'' It is not only the impairment that is important, but how it affects an individual's ability to perform life activities. Three factors are considered in determining whether an impairment substantially limits major life activities:

1. nature and severity
2. how long it will last or is expected to last
3. permanent or long-term impact or expected impact

Major Life Activities

Major life activities are ''activities that an average person can perform with little or no difficulty,'' such as:

- walking
- talking
- breathing
- seeing
- hearing
- learning
- working
- caring for oneself
- lifting
- standing
- performing manual tasks

Sometimes an individual will have more than one impairment, and it is the combination that makes a person ''disabled'' under the ADA.

Record Of An Impairment

Record of an impairment includes people who may have a history of a disability, such as cancer or mental illness. Even though they may not currently have the disability, their history may cause discrimination and they are therefore protected. It also protects people who were misdiagnosed as being disabled.

Regarded As Having An Impairment

Regarded as having an impairment was added to the ADA because, as the Supreme Court has stated and the Congress has reiterated, ''society's myths, fears and stereotypes about disability and disease are as handicapping as are the physical limitations that flow from actual impairments.''

This part of the definition recognizes that an individual may have an impairment that is not substantially limiting, but is treated by an employer as being significant; and that an individual may have an impairment that limits him or her only because of the attitudes of others; or someone may not have an impairment but is regarded as having an impairment.

This is crucial for you to understand, since you, as a supervisor or potential employer, **can make people disabled when they are not.** If you refuse to hire someone for a front-desk receptionist job because the person has facial scars resulting from burns or a birthmark, and cannot show a legitimate, nondiscriminatory reason for your action, you may be in trouble under the ADA.

''But,'' you protest, ''my customers don't want to look at someone with a scarred face!'' The ADA asks us to accept all people into the mainstream of our society, and that means learning to accept people who do not fit the Hollywood definition of attractive. Very few jobs other than professional model require a person to be attractive to successfully perform the essential functions of the position.

Can you think of anyone in your work group who meets any of the above criteria of disabilities?

____

____

> You cannot base an adverse employment decision on unsubstantiated concerns about productivity, safety, insurance, liability, attendance, costs of accommodation, accessibility, workers' compensation costs, or acceptance by co-workers and customers.

This may be one of the most difficult concepts under the ADA to accept, but as a supervisor, you are called upon to make employment decisions based *only* on a person's skills and abilities.

EXCLUSIONS

Drug and alcohol issues are important and somewhat controversial. A person who currently illegally uses drugs is not protected under the ADA. It would be prudent to discuss the latest information on drug and alcohol use and the ADA with your human resources department and with an attorney if you need to take any actions regarding a specific applicant or employee. You may want to read the article, "Drugs, Alcohol and the ADA," by attorney Jonathan A. Segal in the December 1992 issue of *HR Magazine* (pages 73–76).

Physical characteristics such as eye or hair color are not included under ADA protection. Neither are temporary conditions such as broken limbs, colds, flu, and pregnancy unless complications cause more severe conditions. Personality traits such as a quick temper are not ADA-protected. Environmental, cultural or economic disadvantages are not considered to be impairments.

Homosexuality and bisexuality are not considered to be impairments and are therefore not disabilities covered by the ADA. The Act also does not protect sexual and behavioral disorders such as transvestism, compulsive gambling, kleptomania, pyromania, or psychoactive substance use disorders resulting from current illegal use of drugs.

THE IMPACT OF CERTAIN DISABILITIES

How many people are impacted? The U.S. Census Bureau defines ''work disability'' as ''a health problem or disability which prevents you from working or limits the amount or kind of work you can do.''

According to the March 1991 *Current Population Survey*, estimates are that 14,648,000 Americans between 16 and 64 have a work disability. Of those, 29 percent are employed full or part-time, while 71 percent are unemployed.

The National Center for Health Statistics estimates the prevalence of various types of impairments in the U.S. population of all ages:

Impairment	**Number per 1,000 people**
Hearing impairment	94.7
Visual impairment	30.6
Speech impairment	9.3
Arthritis	125.3
Epilepsy	4.8
Missing extremities (excluding toes and fingers)	5.0
Partial/complete paralysis	5.9
Diabetes	25.3
Hypertension	110.2
Heart disease	78.5
Kidney trouble	12.4
Back injury	70.3

(Reported in *In the Mainstream*, November/December 1992, p. 18.)

THE IMPACT OF CERTAIN DISABILITIES (continued)

Other figures from other sources:

- Persons with mental retardation = 1–2 percent of noninstitutionalized population.
- Cerebral palsy = 2 of every 1,000 people.
- Wheelchair users = 1.4 million people.
- Learning disabilities = 12–25 million people.
- Severe long-term mental illness = 2.5 million people.

Current employees may become disabled and eligible for protection under the ADA. Consider how people in your workplace may be impacted by these conditions:

► **Arthritis** is the leading cause of functional limitations in the U.S., affecting 78 of every 1,000 people in the prime working years between ages 45 and 54, and 125 of every 1,000 people of all ages.

► **Heart disease** hits 7 million Americans, 280,000 of whom have bypass surgery by age 45 and then return to work (often being much healthier following surgery than they were before).

► **AIDS** affects many working-age Americans, with one of every four patients between 40 and 49 years old.

► **Chronic low back pain** is most prevalent between ages 45 and 64, and in some professions, is the leading cause of disability.

► **Vision** decreases after age 40, with a number of age-related conditions occurring around age 55.

This should give you some idea of the numbers of people who may benefit from the ADA.

To continue your awareness raising, we will look briefly at some lesser-known disabilities and how they may impact those with whom you work. Keep in mind that ''disabled people come in groups of one, and you can't make generalizations,'' according to Chris Bell, former attorney with the Equal Employment Opportunity Commission.

PHYSICAL DISABILITIES

When we think of the word ''disabled,'' we may picture someone using a wheelchair or a dog guide. We think of a visible physical disability or someone with Down's Syndrome or mental retardation, since it often has physical manifestations. Other disabilities are invisible, such as epilepsy.

Epilepsy deserves specific mention since lack of information contributes to unintentional discrimination against many of the 2 million Americans with the condition. Employers are concerned that an employee with epilepsy may have a seizure on the job. According to Frierson (See Appendix), ''The truth is that most epileptic employees will *never* have a 'fit' or seizure at work. At least 80 percent of all people with epilepsy have the condition completely under control by the use of medication. Many of the 20 percent who occasionally have seizures will tend to have them at night, and even if they occur at work, most seizures are quite mild'' (p. 291). All states now issue driver's licenses to people with epilepsy if they are seizure free.

Epilepsy is the single largest category of impairment leading to lawsuits under the 1973 Rehabilitation Act and similar state laws. If you know that an applicant or employee has epilepsy, learn more about the condition so you can avoid discriminatory employment actions (see Resource Appendix, page 117).

If you know an applicant or employee has a condition with which you are unfamiliar, learn about it before assuming anything about the person's abilities to do (or *not do*) a job.

MENTAL AND EMOTIONAL DISABILITIES

Mental retardation, mental illness, learning disabilities, and traumatic brain injury are often more misunderstood than physical impairments. From early days, we are afraid of people who are labelled "crazy," or "retarded," or "dumb." Until we get to know someone with such a disability, we assume the worst about their capabilities and behaviors. We may fail to consider hiring a person with such a disability because of concerns about productivity, safety, insurance, liability, attendance, and acceptance by co-workers and customers.

As one supervisor of a developmentally disabled person said, "The worst obstacle was fear. Once the fear dissipated, it was easier, and it will be easier for us the next time we hire someone with a disability."

Mental disorders affect about one in five adults, including:

- schizophrenia
- depression
- bipolar disorder
- panic disorders
- obsessive-compulsive disorders

Current members of your work force may have an emotional or mental disorder but may choose to not tell you about it because they may feel you will treat them differently, not consider them for promotion, or will tell co-workers. All of these actions limit the worker's potential and are discriminatory under the ADA. (See Bibliography, page 123, for reference to article by Koglin, Oz, and Hopkins.)

More is being learned all the time about disorders such as schizophrenia, once considered a "split personality." Now it is understood as a disturbance of the processing of information where a person's thoughts may be fragmented, or the ability to properly integrate information may be impaired.

A person with a psychiatric disability may need accommodation to deal with such issues as:

✓ Concentrating

✓ Screening out environmental stimuli

✓ Maintaining stamina through the workday

✓ Managing time pressures and deadlines

✓ Initiating interpersonal contact

✓ Focusing on multiple tasks simultaneously

✓ Responding to negative feedback

✓ Dealing with physical and emotional side effects of medications

For a person with a mental disorder to succeed on the job, supervisors need to maintain a positive attitude about the person's employability, accurately define essential job functions, provide appropriate accommodations, and make sure the employee has full access to all privileges of employment. Note that these are essential characteristics in assuring success of any employee.

Developmental disabilities affect people differently than mental illnesses. Developmental disabilities include Down's syndrome, which results in mental retardation. This simply means that someone learns more slowly than the average. The individual may also lack social skills. However, many employers have found that people with developmental disabilities can be productive workers in a job that suits their skills.

Recognize that learning about disabilities will become part of your supervisory responsibilities. Find out what community agencies can provide information. Start a file into which you put articles or pamphlets.

DISABILITY EDUCATION EXERCISE

I am familiar with the following disabilities and their workplace impact:

____

____

____

I need to learn about these disabilities: ______________________

____

____

____

Sources available for me to learn include: ______________________

____

____

____

My workgroup needs to learn about these disabilities: ____________

____

____

____

I will make these learning opportunities available to my staff: ________

____

____

____

CHRONIC AND PROGRESSIVE CONDITIONS

It is tempting to assume that once a person is disabled, the disability is static, and any accommodations will be made at the beginning of employment. Unfortunately, this is not true since many disabilities change over time. These include arthritis, AIDS, diabetes, some types of vision loss, amyotrophic lateral sclerosis, cancer and others.

Someone who has a past history of cancer may be cured, but is still protected under the ADA under the second part of the definition of a ''qualified individual with a disability'' because discrimination remains. People who return to work after cancer treatments report being:

- ✓ Denied employment
- ✓ Terminated
- ✓ Transferred to different jobs
- ✓ Demoted
- ✓ Denied promotion
- ✓ Refused accommodation
- ✓ Denied fringe benefits

As supervisor, you can educate employees about conditions that cause fear. Invite the American Cancer Society, company doctors, or vocational rehabilitation counselors to present a workshop. The ADA forbids you from disclosing information about a specific employee; however, the person may offer to provide information about his or her condition to co-workers. Fear is usually based on ignorance, but people are generally willing to help co-workers when they understand the circumstances.

Do you have a friend or family member who had difficulty re-entering the workforce? What obstacles did he or she have to overcome?

____

____

____

CHRONIC AND PROGRESSIVE CONDITIONS (continued)

No other aspect of supervision is as difficult as watching a formerly productive employee deal with a progressively worsening physical condition. Some conditions do not improve, but worsen over time.

You need to accommodate the person in any way you can, but you also need to be prepared when he or she is no longer able to do the job and no accommodation will work. Base discussions strictly on the essential functions of the job, asking the employee whether he or she can do those functions, with or without accommodation. Most people will recognize when they can no longer function effectively.

In addition to dealing effectively with the employee, you may need to get support for yourself as well as the employee. Within the limitations of confidentiality, encourage the employee to involve company medical officials or the employee's own medical provider, others who are knowledgeable about the person and his or her disability for support and accurate information. Have someone ''on call'' in case other employees request information or assistance. Use your Employee Assistance Program for support.

Direct Threat

The ADA permits employers to consider ''direct threat'' when making employment decisions. Workers who pose a threat to themselves, co-workers or society do not have to be hired or retained. However, employment decisions must be made on the basis of fact, not myths, stereotypes and outdated information. Reasonable accommodation must also be considered. You must obtain objective evidence that an applicant or employee has recently made threats that implied injury or has committed overt, threatening or harmful acts, then identify the specific risk and behavior posed by the disability.

Fitness for Duty

"Fitness for duty" is another qualification standard to consider. The ADA defines "fitness for duty" as "the degree of risk justifying disqualification that demonstrates reasonable probability of serious or substantial harm." Employment decisions made on this basis must also be based on information from objective data about known risk factors and possible accommodations.

If you make an employment decision based on either of these concerns, you will want to check it with your human resource department or attorney. Remember, the greatest number of lawsuits filed under Title I of the ADA during 1992 were for wrongful discharge.

Attitude Checkpoint

Our favorite supervisors have their opinions of people with disabilities.

Tom Traditional says, "I didn't realize the ADA covered those people who are crazy. I know I don't want any of them in my shop."

Maria Middle-of-the-Road muses, "You mean there may be people in my workgroup now who are disabled? I wonder why they haven't said anything to me. What am I going to do?"

Ann Assertive says, "I'd better make sure I learn as much as I can about disabilities and be aware that any of us could become disabled at any time."

You say, ____

____

____

____

____

____

PART III

Hiring and Involving People with Disabilities

HIRING PEOPLE WITH DISABILITIES

When you have an opening in your department, how do you presently fill it? Do you provide human resources with a current, accurate, written job description that defines the essential functions of the job? Good for you!

Do you have a preconceived notion of the ''type'' of person you want for the job? Does that preconception rule out people who are in any way ''different'' from those who are presently in your workgroup? It is at this point that you will want to expand your horizons, keeping an open mind about the person you hire. Use this as an opportunity to risk having someone new.

Concentrate on what needs to be accomplished, and the skills someone needs, not personality or physical characteristics. Be sure you do not perpetuate stereotypes in written and verbal information. For example, if you have an opening for a front-desk receptionist, rather than asking for a ''young, pleasant-appearing person,'' you will word your announcement something like this: ''need front-office receptionist who makes our customers and clients feel welcome.'' That specifies the *results* you want (customers feeling welcome) rather than the type of person you think can do that.

The key to success with the ADA is understanding the concept of essential functions. The easiest way is to look at your own job. Imagine that you have been selected for a promotion and you are preparing to hire your successor.

EXERCISE

Answer the following:

1. My job exists because ____________________

____

____

____

2. I was hired for my expertise in ____________________

____

____

____

3. The tasks I spend most of my time doing are ____________________

____

____

____

4. If I *did not* do the tasks listed above, this is what would happen ____________________

____

____

____

5. Other duties I perform but which someone else *could* do are ____________________

____

____

____

The tasks you list under items 1–4 above would be considered ''essential functions'' under the ADA, while those in item 5 would be ''marginal.'' The ADA requires that an applicant be able to perform the essential functions of a job, with or without reasonable accommodation.

JOB ANALYSIS

What you have just done is complete the first part of a ''job analysis.'' You will need to analyze all jobs and incorporate your analysis in the job descriptions. In addition to identifying essential and marginal functions, complete the following for your own job.

✓ **Physical requirements** ______________________________

____

✓ **Mental requirements** ______________________________

____

✓ **Working conditions** ______________________________

____

✓ **Level of responsibility** ______________________________

____

✓ **Layout of work station and building** ______________________________

____

✓ **Accessibility of bathroom and areas used by all employees, such as eating areas, training rooms, health clubs, and parking** ______________________________

____

✓ **Equipment used to do the job: i.e., milling machine, carpenter's tools, computer, laboratory equipment** ______________________________

____

JOB ANALYSIS (continued)

More complete methods of conducting job analysis include checklists or computer programs that might be available from your human resources department.

This exercise gets you started thinking about jobs so you can logically review them to determine their components. Then you can hire someone who will be successful.

Now, using the essential functions you wrote, develop a job announcement for your job. Write the information for a job announcement below:

JOB DESCRIPTION EXERCISE

Job title: ______________________________

What results do you expect? ______________________________

____

____

What are the essential functions of the job? ______________________________

____

____

What education, certification or licenses are required? ______________________________

____

____

What must the person do to apply? ______________________________

____

____

POSTING JOB ANNOUNCEMENTS

As you begin to write job announcements in this way, you will open your mind to hiring people for their *skills* rather than discounting characteristics such as physical or mental disabilities. This is the whole point of the ADA.

After you have written your job announcement, then what?

The ADA requires that announcements be available and accessible to all applicants. Check to ensure that yours are at a height where anyone can access them, that they are in a language that all employees can understand, and that they are available to people who do not read well. If job announcements are only available in written format, and the job does not require reading, you may be unwittingly discriminating against someone who doesn't read. You may put them on tape or in a voice mail box or have someone available to read them aloud.

Make sure, also, that you have posted the appropriate ADA notices, either in your employment office or department, as required by the ADA.

There is more to recruiting potential employees, but we will assume that your human resources department utilizes community organizations and schools to identify qualified candidates with disabilities. We will concentrate on the activities of a typical supervisor.

ASSESSING APPLICANTS' ABILITY TO DO THE JOB

What you are attempting to determine, both in your review of a person's application and during the assessment process, is whether the person is *qualified* to do the job. There are many ways, in addition to the traditional interview, to get accurate information.

> *Qualified* as defined by the ADA means that a person has the requisite education, training, licenses, background and experience to do the job.

This is your goal in assessing any person, disabled or not. You are also trying to identify what makes one candidate stand out among all of them.

Effectively assessing any job applicant is both an art and a science. You are trying to find someone who can:

- Perform specific job tasks
- Fit into the organizational culture
- Get along well as a team player
- Be punctual and regular in attendance
- Be pleasant about doing what needs to be done

Depending on the job and the state of the economy, you may have more applicants than you can possibly interview, or not enough who have the skills you seek. You want to get the best person as fast as possible and with as little disruption as possible. You may want a person who can hit the ground running and not require much of your time for training.

How often do you find the perfect candidate? Even after reviewing many resumes, you may not find the one person who meets all your needs. Almost all people will require some training and some period of adjustment. Co-workers may have difficulty accepting a new team member, especially one who does not fit the mold of previous team members. If the work group has traditionally been all male, or all white, or all physically able, you and others may have a period of adjustment. So, do not let the presence of a disability influence your decision making or the way you evaluate an applicant with a disability.

You will want to use legal and effective methods to determine a person's appropriateness for a job. These include . . .

- checking references, including school references for people with little or no work experience
- internships
- testing
- on-the-job evaluations
- job tryouts

Develop three ways to assess a person's ability to do your job.

1. ______________________________

____

____

____

2. ______________________________

____

____

____

3. ______________________________

____

____

____

CONDUCTING INTERVIEWS

If you have not attended training on current interviewing practices and laws, you may want to do so. Interviewing can be a minefield of potential problems, not only those related to disability. The Equal Employment Opportunity Commission has prepared general guidelines of acceptable and unacceptable interview questions. You may find reviewing this information beneficial. Your HR department should also provide guidance.

One way to keep yourself out of trouble is to ask yourself, before asking any question in an interview, ''What is the purpose of this question?'' If you focus only on information necessary to make a hiring decision, you reduce your chance of asking something illegal.

However, it is difficult to imagine that two human beings are *exactly* the same. If two people appear to have the same background, education and experience, then you would need to determine which one will ''fit'' the requirements of the job better. You can ask the two candidates questions that will demonstrate their differences in problem solving, communication, or other job-related skills. You can ask open-ended questions such as, ''I have several well-qualified candidates for this job. Please tell me what you bring to this job that would make you the person I should hire.'' You can also ask questions such as ''what would your past employer say if we asked what your greatest contribution to the organization was?'' **Caution:** Be sure that your questions remain *job related* and do not deal with real or perceived disabilities.

What if I have two candidates who are equally qualified? Must I hire the person with the disability over the other?

The answer in this case is NO! The ADA is not an ''affirmative action law.'' It is a ''nondiscrimination law,'' which requires only that we not discriminate on the basis of our perceptions about a person's disability.

Be careful in interviewing people who are new to the job market or who may not have worked since the onset of a disability. The new person may not have a significant track record to refer to, and the newly disabled person may have changed significantly since the last job.

In addition to not questioning people about their present disabilities, you cannot ask about previous workers' compensation claims, history of hospitalizations or past substance abuse. You may not ask how often a person will need to be absent for medical care. However, you *can* state your company's attendance policies and ask if the person can meet them.

Group Interviewing

Perhaps you have work teams interview candidates. In this case, you need to train team members about which questions are appropriate and helpful and which are irrelevant. Irrelevant questions are those which provide no useful information. One person asking one illegal question can put the company in jeopardy for a lawsuit. Team members also need to become aware of the need for increased confidentiality about candidates.

Teams can legally and appropriately ask candidates about how they solve problems, how they work in a team, what their leadership experiences have been, and so forth. A good question may be to ask how the candidate determines the success of a work team.

Work teams are designed to brainstorm and solve problems. If a person has lived with a disability for a long time, he or she has probably had ample experience in evaluating situations and determining appropriate ways to deal with them, a skill which the team would find valuable.

HIRING AND ADA COMPLIANCE

The ADA is complex and comprehensive, covering all aspects of employment, from advertising job announcements to interviewing, providing reasonable accommodations, and supervising, training and promoting employees with disabilities. Each facet of employment must be covered in training.

Attitude Checkpoint

Our three supervisors each have a job opening in their department. Let's check with them to see how they communicate the requirements of the position.

Tammy Traditional states she is looking for a ''cheerful, pleasant-looking person'' to fill her secretarial job opening.

Maria Middle-of-the-Road states she is looking for a secretary who is ''pleasant looking and who can handle the pressure of a lot of phone calls.''

Ann Assertive states she is looking for a secretary who can ''type 50 words-per-minute, handle a lot of phone calls, and makes clients feel welcome.''

Your job announcement states that you need someone who: ________

____

____

____

____

____

INVOLVING PEOPLE WITH DISABILITIES

The supervisor sets the tone for a work group. If you are fearful and hesitant about workplace changes, you will communicate that fear to the group. If, however, you deal effectively with change, you will inspire a more positive feeling to your workers. This is especially true when it comes to emotional issues such as sexual harassment and dealing with people with disabilities.

Establishing a Culture of Acceptance and Productivity

Think about how you establish the tone for your work area. Circle the word in each pair that most closely describes your work group.

- calm or hurried
- casual or formal
- playful or serious

How does the tone affect relationships and productivity? Is your area known to go along with the rest of the organization, or is it seen as a maverick? Do people get along well, or is there dissention? Is productivity as high as it should be?

A key question is, how are people who are "different" treated? Are people accepted only for what they can do for the bottom line? Is everyone included in social events? Do people interact with everyone in the group, or only with those of the same sex, race or cultural background?

These are important considerations as the workplace becomes more diverse. To be effective, an organization and the units within it must accept and include all who contribute to the bottom line. This extends to those with physical or mental differences as well as gender or ethnic differences.

INVOLVING PEOPLE WITH DISABILITIES (continued)

If someone from outside your organization were to ask you to describe what it is like to work in your department, what words would you use to describe the culture of the area?

____

____

What is your organization doing, and what are you doing, as the supervisor, to create an atmosphere of acceptance for all employees and encourage effective interaction?

____

____

One way for a supervisor to help employees be more comfortable with people with disabilities as colleagues and co-workers is to provide sensitivity training *before* the need arises. Training in a ''safe'' environment allows people to make mistakes in a learning setting rather than in a situation that may result in discomfort or a lawsuit.

What should such training cover?

✓ Types of disabilities and their functional limitations

✓ Language about and around people with disabilities

✓ Communication skills

✓ Offering assistance

✓ Confidentiality

✓ Role playing

✓ Involving people with disabilities in the training to help employees become comfortable

SENSITIVITY AND AWARENESS

Our minds create fears within us about dealing with people with disabilities. In addition, most of us have had little or no experience in dealing with them. We have, therefore, no frame of reference, and little or no experience in communicating appropriately. We do not know how to offer and provide assistance graciously, tactfully and effectively. In addition, we have the pressure to not make a "mistake" that will get us into legal trouble. It is no wonder that we are frightened of our first encounter with a person with a disability!

Most organizations have focused on ADA compliance training for policy makers, managers and supervisors. However, because of people's fears of disabilities and misunderstandings about the capabilities of people with disabilities, ADA compliance training meets only half the training need. Unless an organization provides disability awareness and sensitivity training, employees will be resistant to full implementation of the ADA.

Why should the training include people with disabilities? ____________________

____

____

____

____

____

We are talking about new ways of communicating and interacting with people. This is not theoretical, textbook stuff. Trainees need to practice new behaviors, not just in role playing, but with real people to get over their real fears and hesitations.

If you are training other supervisors or people who interview job applicants, be sure to include role play of this situation. Practice using a sign language interpreter if you foresee the possibility of hiring a person who is deaf. Once people have practiced in this situation, they are more comfortable and confident. Contact a local service center for deaf people for a list of registered interpreters.

FINDING AWARENESS TRAINING RESOURCES

Organizations can contract with independent consultants who are themselves disabled; however, do not assume that just because a person is disabled, he or she knows how to conduct such training. As you would with any other consultant, be sure to get references and find out how effective the previous training has been. Several references are listed in the Resources section in the Appendix.

Present employees with disabilities are often willing to share their experiences to enlighten their co-workers. They can either formally or informally educate others about their specific conditions, or other disabilities.

What awareness training needs to be done in your work group?

____

____

____

You may ask employers who have had successful experiences in employing people with disabilities to answer questions about their experiences. Many organizations that represent the interests of people with disabilities will provide training at little or no cost as a public service. There are numerous videos available pertaining to employees with disabilities. However, videos are not good substitutes for actually talking to people with disabilities face to face. It helps employees in an organization to recognize that people with disabilities are people first. Nothing helps erase the stereotypes and myths about people with disabilities more readily than the experience of spending time with them informally.

Training in these skills will help ensure that employees are more sensitive, will accept co-workers with disabilities more readily, and all employees will be more productive. While training cannot by itself eliminate fears and stereotypes, providing appropriate training on both compliance and attitudes about people with disabilities shows commitment to incorporating qualified employees with disabilities into an organization. It helps current employees look at their attitudes and begin to accept the changes the ADA will bring.

COMMUNICATING WITH DISABLED EMPLOYEES

What is appropriate when talking with employees with disabilities? Some hints:

- Focus on work related topics and the same things that you discuss with nondisabled employees. *Remember, a person is more than his or her disability.* The disability is unimportant unless you are discussing reasonable accommodations.

- In social situations, discuss the same things you discuss with anyone. Weather, sports, movies, politics and current events are all appropriate. It is important that employees with disabilities are included in an organization's social activities, since work-related discussions often occur there.

- Communicating with an employee who is hard of hearing or deaf may be a new experience for you. It is OK to admit that you need to learn.

    - You will want to discuss with the person early in the employment how she or he prefers to communicate. Many people with diminished hearing use a combination of methods to understand spoken language, including speechreading and interpreting body language. This may be combined with quickly jotting down key words or phrases. It is a misconception that a person can understand everything you say by reading your lips. Even an excellent speechreader can accurately comprehend less than half of what is said. Augment this with other forms of communication.

    - To let a person who is deaf or hard of hearing know that you wish to speak with him or her, you may touch the person gently on the shoulder or elbow. Ask he or she early on how they would like you to do that to avoid any misperception of your intentions.

- Do not shout at a person who is blind unless you know that the person also has a hearing impairment.

- Speak normally. It is OK to say, ''Do you see what I mean?'' to a person who is blind, even if the person cannot see anything. Everyone uses figures of speech such as this.

COMMUNICATING WITH DISABLED EMPLOYEES (continued)

- It is courteous to pull up a chair, sit down, and face a person who uses a wheelchair when you are having more than a brief conversation. You would not want to have to look up at everyone you speak to all day. In addition, it evens the power between the two of you.

- It is especially important to communicate effectively with employees with developmental disabilities. Do not talk ''baby talk'' to them. Break down complex instructions into small tasks. Use alternative forms of job instruction such as color coding or pictures. Ask them to repeat instructions to you or demonstrate their understanding of your instructions. Other employees who are patient and are interested in seeing a developmentally disabled worker succeed can assist in providing instructions and feedback.

- Just as you would with any employee, treat people with disabilities as individuals. All people who are blind people are not the same, neither are all people who are sighted. Do not generalize about people based on their disability.

When in doubt, remember the Golden Rule: ''Do unto others as you would have them do unto you,'' and the 3 C's—Courtesy, Communication and Common Sense!

UNDERSTANDING DISABILITY CULTURES

Being a person with a disability is more than having a physical or mental impairment that substantially limits daily activities. In many cases, it involves a way of life and a philosophy. It may mean belonging to an organization of others who have that disability such as the National Federation of the Blind. It may mean separation, such as attending a church for people who are deaf or participating in Special Olympics.

These are organizations based on similarities. All of us enjoy belonging to organizations based on our interests. Some belong to a sports league, while others participate in service clubs. Each of these organizations has a culture with ceremonies, traditions and customs.

In addition, we may attend support groups for common life experiences, such as Al-Anon or a support group for those who recently went through a divorce. These are resources we call upon to deal with new experiences in our lives.

Each of these groups has a culture that we may not understand if we are an "outsider." However much we try, we cannot understand or "belong." This may be true of an employee with a disability. There are "deaf cultures," "blind cultures," and cultures of other disability groups.

As a supervisor, you learn all you can about your workgroup members. You may study someone's cultural background or learn sign language. You may read about the impact of divorce. But unless you have firsthand experience, you will probably never understand the complexities of these situations.

When any employee has problems on the job, you try to understand the basis for those problems in order to help the employee solve them. You refer them to your Employee Assistance Program or an appropriate community resource agency. It is the same with an employee with a disability. You may need to refer yourself to a group that understands disability culture. There are professional associations, such as the National Association of the Deaf, which can help you understand the culture represented by an employee who is disabled.

To find organizations that can help you, first ask employees with disabilities or look in your local telephone directory. You can also contact Independent Living Centers for people with disabilities for referrals to appropriate local organizations. The *ADA Technical Assistance Manual* lists national offices of numerous organizations.

Understanding your employees is an attribute that makes you successful as a supervisor.

USING APPROPRIATE LANGUAGE

What is the difference between the words ''*handicapped*'' and ''*disabled*''?

While not everyone agrees, most people in the various disability communities prefer to use the word *disability* when discussing physical conditions. *Handicap* is the barrier that society puts up, either a physical barrier that prevents a person with a mobility impairment from entering a store or an attitudinal barrier that limits a person from becoming employed. For example, ''The steps *handicapped* the young woman, who had a *disability*, from getting into the building.''

We may be accustomed to speaking about people with disabilities as ''handicapped'' or lumping them with others who have the same disability, such as ''the blind.'' It is more appropriate to emphasize the *person* instead of assigning the person to a group based only on one characteristic. If you must talk about a person by identifying the disability, remember to say, ''the *person* who is . . . '' (blind, deaf, a wheelchair user, etc.).

Rather than referring to someone as ''the blind man,'' you may say, ''the new accountant.'' ''Why,'' you ask, ''not let people know he is blind?'' It is more appropriate to refer to people by their names, but if you *must* identify them by a disability, you may say, ''the accountant who is blind.''

Why is this important? We know that language influences action, and because of negative stereotypes and expectations about people with disabilities, using inappropriate language may influence inappropriate actions. For example, referring to someone as ''wheelchair bound'' creates a picture in our mind of someone who never leaves the wheelchair and may not be able to move about effectively in the workplace. It may influence our decision about whether or not to hire the person for a job that requires travel out of the office. A wheelchair is nothing more than an assistive device that allows a person to use something other than legs to move about. If we think of it as an assistive device rather than something that ''binds'' someone to something, we will not make assumptions about what that device permits a person to do.

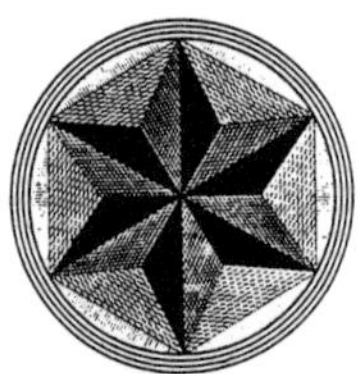 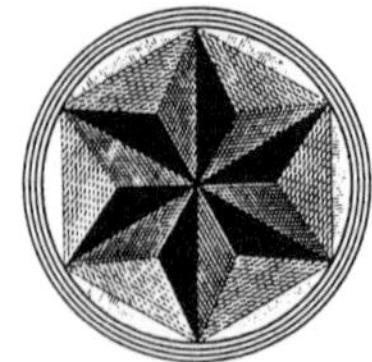 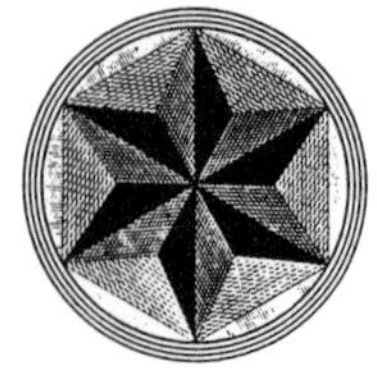

INCORPORATING PEOPLE WITH DISABILITIES

In 1975, Congress passed a law called "The Education of All Handicapped Children's Act." It is also called "Public Law 94-142," or the "Mainstreaming Law." It was reauthorized in 1991 and is now known as the "Individuals with Disabilities Education Act" (IDEA).

This law offers children with disabilities an education in the "least restrictive environment" rather than automatically being sent to special schools or special classrooms. The idea is that all children, both those with disabilities and those without, could benefit from learning in the same classroom.

What does this have to do with the ADA?

Children who were in first grade in 1975 were born about 1970, making them 22 in 1992, the year Title I of the ADA took effect for larger companies. They may just be entering the work force. Let's look at the various groups this may affect.

► **Young people with disabilities** educated for all or part of their schooling under this law might:

- Be accustomed to being with nondisabled colleagues in school activities from the classroom to the choir
- Have had accommodations made for their disability
- Know more about their rights and responsibilities under various laws such as the ADA
- Have higher expectations of themselves and their employers

► **Nondisabled people who had disabled classmates** may have had different, and probably more positive, experiences than those of us who grew up with no disabled classmates. They might:

- Be more accepting, less fearful, and more aware that people with disabilities can get along and be productive
- Know more about accommodations

To them, co-workers with disabilities may be "no big deal."

INCORPORATING PEOPLE WITH DISABIITIES (continued)

► **Employees in your workgroup who are parents of children with disabilities born after 1970** may also be more aware and accepting. They may:

- Have been active in getting their schools to accommodate their disabled child
- Be familiar with suppliers and funding sources of reasonable accommodation
- Have been creating adaptations and accommodations for their children, and can be valuable resources in suggesting workplace accommodations
- Have a vested interest in seeing the workplace become more accessible, since their children with disabilities will someday enter the workforce

People with disabilities, both young and old, can help provide positive experiences from which those without disabilities can learn. Without being "brave," or "amazing," but by being productive on the job, they can help those who doubt learn that people with disabilities can be valuable members of the workforce.

Supervisors would be smart to tap the experiences and wisdom of all these people in their workforce.

Attitude Checkpoint

A memo comes around that says:

> *To all employees: The Americans with Disabilities Act of 1990 prohibits discrimination on the basis of disability. This company supports the premise that all qualified people, regardless of sex, race, national origin, religion, or disability, shall be given an equal opportunity to use their skills and abilities in our workplace. You will receive further information about this law. In the meantime, please recognize that we stand ready to comply with the ADA to the fullest extent.*

Tom Traditional says: ''Why don't those people stay home where they belong? I don't have time to babysit someone who can't meet our production standards.''

Mark Middle-of-the-Road says: ''Well, maybe there aren't that many disabled people out there. Maybe none of them will want to work here.''

Ann Assertive says, ''We've been having trouble finding good workers. I went to highschool with this guy in a wheelchair. He was great at math. I hear he went on to college and became an accountant. I wonder whatever happened to him.''

You say: ____

____

____

____

____

____

PART

IV

Managing and Enhancing the Performance of People with Disabilities

MANAGING AND PROMOTING PEFORMANCE

Managers today have many tools and opportunities to support and promote top-notch performance from all employees.

Training

It is important to encourage all your employees to develop their talents through additional training and challenging assignments that offer them opportunities to stretch and grow. Work with your training department to ensure that all training is offered in accessible locations and that materials are provided in accessible formats.

Provide adequate on-the-job training for all employees, ensuring that training materials are in accessible formats and that appropriate time is given for people to learn the job.

Providing Feedback

The ADA does not require that you lower quality or quantity standards for any employee. You must communicate effectively with all employees about your expectations. You may supervise someone who has not worked before. You will need to communicate your expectations just as you would with any other new and inexperienced employee. You have the opportunity to help the person develop untested work skills and attitudes that will be the basis for the rest of his or her working life. The individual will remember his first supervisor more favorably, and later supervisors will applaud your efforts at helping a new member of the workforce develop appropriate skills and work attitudes.

Workers with disabilities need feedback on their performance just like other employees, praise when appropriate and corrective counseling or coaching when needed. Do not wait until there is a serious problem. Involve the employee in problem-solving discussions before the situation becomes job-threatening.

PROVIDING FEEDBACK (continued)

If a person with a disability is performing below standards, supervisors and co-workers become increasingly more frustrated that the disabled employee is not contributing. If *any* member of a work team is incompetent or not performing to full capacity, others must take up the slack. Resentment builds, and soon, that person, along with *all* people with disabilities, is unwelcome as a co-worker and employee.

When reviewing the performance of an employee with a disability, it is especially important to focus on the outcome of the employee's work. Describe the behavior or work outcome and solicit input from the employee about how the problem can be resolved. Be prepared to accommodate the person if necessary. This does **not** necessarily mean to accept lower quality or quantity from the person.

Do not assume that performance problems are automatically disability related.

Conducting Performance Appraisals

A supervisor once said, ''Oh, I never do a performance appraisal on my disabled employees. It's enough that, with their disabilities, they are here and try hard. It wouldn't be fair to do a performance appraisal.'' Although you may be required to do a performance appraisal, how often do you look at effort instead of results? If a person with a disability has the skills necessary to work, does it not make sense to evaluate the performance? Is it fair (or legal?) to deny the person feedback that could lead to improved performance and opportunities for advancement?

Use the job description, with its delineation of essential functions, as a basis for performance appraisal. (This justifies the time you spend conducting the job analysis and writing the job description! Everything ties together in a neat package.)

Generally, performance appraisals are conducted by an employee's supervisor; however, some organizations successfully combine supervisory review with peer review and/or self-evaluation.

While appraisals generally review a person's past performance, done correctly, they can be a good counseling tool to help an employee improve and grow in the job.

CASE STUDY #1

You hired Sally, a wheelchair user, as a word processing specialist. She has been on the job for six months and you are reviewing her performance. You tell her that she is not producing the number of documents required of others working in the department for the same length of employment. Also, her documents contain some spelling errors. You and Sally leave the meeting frustrated.

CASE STUDY REVIEW

What might you say about this performance appraisal?

- Let's go back to the beginning of Sally's employment. Did you provide her with an adequate job description that included the expected standards of quantity required after the initial period? Did you provide her with a list of some of the unusual words in your industry or company and make sure that she had a good dictionary or spellcheck program?

- Did you talk with Sally about any needs to accommodate the limitations imposed by her disability? For example, is her keyboard at an ergonomically correct height and position for her? Did you ask her if her work station is set up for maximum productivity?

- During the performance appraisal, did you provide Sally with specific standards for both the quantity of documents she is to produce as well as the acceptable number of errors? Did you ask her how she feels about her performance and what she needs from you to do her job better?

- Did you set a short time period to check back with her about improvements?

As you can see, dealing with performance problems and conducting a performance appraisal for a person with a disability is similar to the process for any employee.

IMPROVING WORK-GROUP RELATIONS

Managers today have the challenge of supervising an increasingly diverse workgroup. With the increasingly common blend of cultures—men, women, and people with disabilities—a few guidelines will make everyone feel more comfortable, and improve relations among everyone.

Limiting Unwanted "Helpfulness"

Most employees are helpful to each other. If employees have not worked with a person with a disability in the past, they may stumble all over themselves (and the co-worker) trying to be helpful. You may need to prevent well-meaning but uninformed people from providing unneeded and unwanted assistance. Remind co-workers that the new person was hired because he or she had the skills to do the job. Most people with disabilities will tell people if and when they need help.

Dog guides used by people with visual, hearing, or mobility impairments are especially susceptible to "over-helpfulness." Employees must learn that the dog is there to work, not to play or eat. Distracting a dog guide that is in harness can be dangerous to the user, since the person depends on the dog to avoid obstacles. The employee may need to educate co-workers about relating to the dog. Once the novelty of having a dog in the workplace wears off, most people interact appropriately.

Maintaining Confidentiality

The ADA requires strict confidentiality about any employee's disability. Only supervisors and emergency personnel are permitted access to this information. People are curious, however, and will want to know "what's wrong" with the new person. You need to explain that everyone is hired on the basis of *a*bility, not *dis*ability, and that you cannot answer personal questions. Most people understand when you tell them that you would respect personal information about them.

MAINTAINING CONFIDENTIALITY (continued)

It is important for employees to be aware that they or a disabled co-worker may need reasonable accommodation, *and* that the confidentiality requirements of the ADA may preclude co-workers from knowing why accommodation is being made. This is a crucial issue, especially in small, tightly knit work groups where everyone usually knows everything about everyone else.

If an employee with a disability chooses to educate co-workers about the disability, that becomes an individual choice. However, you cannot require such personal disclosures.

Understanding Cultural Differences

No other country has a law as inclusive of people with disabilities as the United States. This is partially because other cultures have different views of people with disabilities than we do.

- In some cultures, a person who is born ''deformed'' is left to die at birth.
- In others, the person with a disability is seen as an outcast or a demon.
- In many, the family is expected to take care of the person in the home for his or her entire lifetime, and the person may never leave the home.
- In some countries, people with severe disabilities live in government-run institutions.

With the influx of so many new workers, the cultural beliefs that people from other cultures carry may be brought into America's organizations. If a person from another culture comes to this country, becomes a productive worker, and is confronted with a person with a disability, what issues might come up?

- fear
- mistrust
- feeling that the person with a disability doesn't belong
- communication problems
- discrimination

These may look familiar, since they are the same ones that we all face.

As the supervisor, you need to be aware of the potential for problems related to cultural background. As part of diversity training, you will want to discuss various cultural perceptions of disability, and let everyone know what the ADA says about our own cultural willingness to involve persons with a disability in the mainstream of American life. Most workers from other cultures will obey our laws, but they may need help in understanding why they feel the way they do.

Promoting Inclusion

Social isolation may be a problem for an employee with a disability. Because so many people are unaccustomed to having co-workers with disabilities, they may hesitate to include them in coffee breaks, lunches, office parties, sporting events, the company picnic and Christmas party, and other social events.

Let's go back to Sally, the word processor whose work you reviewed in the performance appraisal. You observe that she doesn't seem to "fit in" very well. She doesn't socialize with others. You ask her if she is trying, and she says, "yes."

Ask yourself some questions:

- Did you provide training to your other employees about the ADA and about the capabilities of people with disabilities?

- Did you introduce Sally to others in the department and encourage them to include her in lunch and coffee breaks?

You need to create an atmosphere, not just of acceptance, but of inclusion, where all workers are included in all activities and valued for their contribution.

Including Employees with Disabilities in Work Teams

Supervisors may be concerned about how people with disabilities will fit into quality teams, task forces, or employee committees. The answer is, they will probably fit in well and use their skills to benefit the group. Having a team member with a disability will provide another perspective for problem solving and ideas for quality improvement.

Work teams that perform interdependent tasks may improve interaction among members. This can improve chances for an employee with a disability to become infused into the work group rather than being isolated. Self-managed work groups can also use their skills to develop needed accommodations.

List three specific benefits to your workgroup of including people with disabilities in work teams.

1. ____

____

____

2. ____

____

____

3. ____

____

____

OTHER MANAGEMENT CONSIDERATIONS

Involving the Employee

If a person is skilled enough to be in the workplace, he or she is probably skilled enough to make decisions. One of the key concepts of the ADA is self-determination and involvement. If job duties change or problems come up, involve the person and avoid making assumptions about needs. Do not feel that you have to have all the answers—someone who lives with a disability makes decisions daily. If outside assistance is necessary, make the employee with the disability part of the team.

Handling Emergencies

Discuss emergency evacuation and safety procedures with your employees with disabilities. Ask about their experiences in previous jobs. If this is a new experience or significantly different from the past, you may want to get guidance from your human resources, first aid, or safety officer.

Examples of issues which require advance planning . . .

- Fire drills and evacuation procedures for wheelchair users, people with hearing and visual limitations, and people with developmental disabilities. If your department is on an upper floor, elevators would not be available to anyone in an emergency. There are several ways to creatively deal with the situation, each with potential problems. Do not assume that co-workers want or should have the responsibility for carrying a wheelchair user down several flights of stairs. Liability issues may arise if either person should gets hurt from improper carrying.

- People with developmental disabilities may need to practice emergency evacuation procedures more frequently than others. Discuss training with organizations such as the Association for Retarded Citizens or vocational rehabilitation agencies, which provide training for clients with these disabilities for ideas on how to prepare for emergencies.

If you have employees who are supported by an outside agency, involve the job coach in training.

OTHER MANAGEMENT CONSIDERATIONS (continued)

Taking Disciplinary Action and Dismissal

Sometimes, it becomes necessary to terminate an employee with a disability. As with any termination, it can be painful for all involved. It is especially difficult, and potentially more questionable from a legal standpoint, if the supervisor did not communicate performance problems to the employee. The person with a disability may or may not be aware of problems. If he or she is unaware, being let go is even more devastating, since it happens unexpectedly.

It is challenging for a supervisor to take disciplinary action or terminate any employee. Some supervisors have said that they do not want to hire a person with a disability because they wouldn't have the heart to fire them. Unfortunately, sometimes there is not a good match between a person and a job, or interpersonal concerns get in the way, or any one of a number of things can happen that make discipline, or perhaps termination, necessary.

You must use the same criteria to discipline or terminate an employee with a disability as any other employee. Document poor performance, attempts at coaching, and all efforts to accommodate the limitations imposed by the disability. But *do not* automatically assume that performance problems are caused by the disability.

If an agency such as vocational rehabilitation was involved in the hiring of the person, you may want to call the person with whom you worked before taking any final action. Sometimes a third party can suggest alternatives that will solve the problem.

As with any situation like this, you will want to involve your human resources or legal department to ensure that emotions are not getting in the way of judgement and that you are following proper procedures.

If an employee leaves voluntarily, you will want to take the same precautions that you would take with any other employee; i.e., do not get angry, include the person in meetings to which he or she should be invited while still there, do not withhold information, etc.

Preparing People with Disabilities for Promotion

The ADA covers *all* employment situations, not just hiring. Underemployment of people with disabilities is a continuing problem. Recognize that employees with disabilities who are serious about their careers are as interested in career development as anyone else. Just because a person is good at one level does not necessarily mean that he or she wants to stay at that level or at that job.

Have you conducted a skills inventory of all your employees so you know who has additional skills? Do you cross-train your staff so that they are versatile in the job tasks they can perform? There are many advantages, including being able to restructure jobs to accommodate an employee with a disability.

Make sure that all your employees, including those with disabilities receive notices of training and promotional opportunities. Encourage professional development activities such as membership in trade associations, speaking at conferences, or publishing articles in professional journals.

Attitude Checkpoint

How might our three supervisors conduct a performance appraisal of an employee with a disability?

Tammy Traditional would probably not conduct an appraisal. She feels that it is enough that the employee works at all and she feels very uncomfortable with the thought that she might need to discuss a situation that needs performance improvement.

Maria Middle-of-the-Road would probably delay as long as possible conducting the performance appraisal. When she did the appraisal, she would focus on the positive performance—which every good supervisor should do—but she would gloss over or not mention areas needing improvement.

Andy Assertive provides timely, thoughtful, and thorough performance appraisals for his entire staff. He and a human resource representative designed a standard appraisal form that he uses with all his employees to provide each person with quantifiable standards of performance. He provides objective and supportive feedback to each employee within each person's written job description.

You would: ____

____

____

____

____

____

ENHANCING EMPLOYEE PRODUCTIVITY

How do we enhance our current employees' ability to do their job?

☐ We purchase equipment that increases productivity, such as word processors instead of typewriters.

☐ We offer chairs with back supports to workers who must sit all day.

☐ We may provide flextime to accommodate the needs of working parents.

☐ We offer employee assistance programs to help workers deal with personal problems.

Some workplace modifications cost almost nothing, while others are expensive. However, we consider the employees' health and welfare to be crucial in their ability to meet our needs as employers. We absorb the cost as a cost of doing business.

What do you presently do to enhance worker productivity in your organization?

____

____

____

Modifications for Employee Productivity

The same philosophy applies to providing reasonable accommodations for workers with disabilities.

The purpose of accommodating qualified people with disabilities is to enhance their abilities so that, despite the disability, they are productive. We need only to accommodate limitations in their ability to perform the essential functions of the job. The modifications cannot cause our organization an "undue hardship." Determining undue hardship is best left to senior policy makers in your company. As a supervisor you need to concentrate on looking at how to determine reasonable accommodations.

MODIFICATIONS FOR EMPLOYEE PRODUCTIVITY (continued)

Keep in mind that you only need to accommodate a *known* disability. You are not expected to be a physician or psychologist who diagnoses disabilities. If the employee asks for an accommodation, or if the person has a noticeable disability that appears to limit his or her ability to do the essential functions, you need to consider accommodations.

Accommodation is a collaborative process between the employee and the supervisor. Do not automatically assume that an employee with a disability needs accommodation or that accommodations must be fancy or expensive. Some require only an attitudinal adjustment on the part of supervisors and co-workers. In each case, consider:

- job duties
- work environment
- limitations imposed by the disability
- other employees doing the same job
- safety issues
- financial implications

The first step is to insure that an employee with a mobility impairment can get into the building and access the work area. Beyond that, examples of accommodation include:

► **Job restructuring**—Pat, a file clerk who is deaf, cannot answer the telephone; therefore she takes on additional duties, such as ordering office supplies, while another clerk answers the phone. A danger to guard against in this situation is using the phrase, ''But, we've always done it this way!''

► **Part-time or modified work schedule**—Diego, a wheelchair user, comes to work 1/2 hour earlier (or later) than other employees to take advantage of accessible public transportation.

- **Reassignment to a vacant position**—Dale, an employee injured on the job, returns to the same company, but in a different job.

- **Acquisition or modification of equipment or devices**—Kieko, a drafter who uses a wheelchair, needs her desk raised so her wheelchair will fit under it. A 2×4 is placed under each leg of her desk. This may make the desk surface too high, so additional adjustments are made to keep the workstation ergonomically correct.

- **Adjustment or modification of examinations, training materials or policies**—Olaf, a management trainee who has diabetes, attends a week-long training program. He must eat small snacks and administer his insulin on a regular basis, so is provided a small ice chest and regularly scheduled breaks.

- **Provision of qualified readers or interpreters**—A secretary reads daily mail to Tan, a blind computer programmer. An interpreter serves so a deaf employee can participate fully in staff meetings.

- **Other, similar accommodations for individuals with disabilities**—Susan, who is undergoing treatmet for breast cancer, leaves early one day a week for chemotherapy treatments.

If you have quality improvement teams, and **if** the employee with a disability is willing, team members may brainstorm ways to accommodate the disability. In the process, they may well determine an improvement that would assist all team members to be more productive. This is just a different form of problem solving and managing for quality.

Often, you will find that an accommodation for one person's disability actually helps other employees. It may also help customers and others who do business with you. For example, installing a ramp for a wheelchair user makes it easier for delivery people and parents with baby strollers. Ramps are also easier to shovel after a snowstorm than steps.

Disability Accommodation Flow Chart

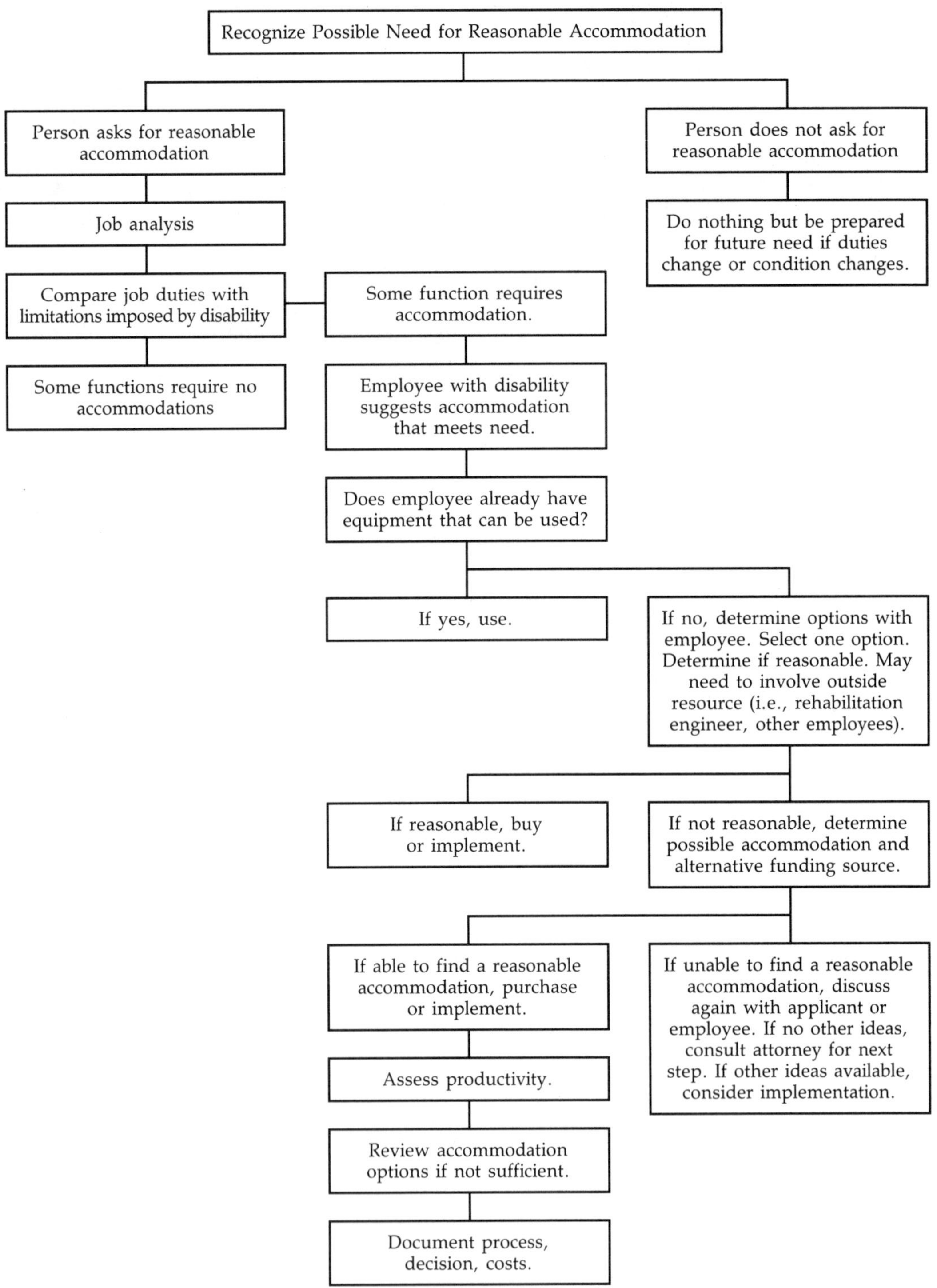

APPLYING CREATIVITY AND ADAPTABILITY

In today's changing environments, supervisors must be flexible, accepting new information, methods, and workforce members. They must meet the major pressures on their time and energy and remain focused.

A key criteria for success in supervision and enhanced employee productivity is **CREATIVITY**. Dealing with unknown situations, whether they are new equipment purchase policies or human resource initiatives, requires the ability to step out of your comfort zone and look at these opportunities from a new perspective. Reading is not enough. You need an experience that will show you how creative you can be. Let's consider a fun yet practical application of the principles of reasonable accommodation.

CASE STUDY #2

You have been invited to the home of a new business colleague who has recently arrived from Japan. You have never before eaten with chopsticks. A delicious meal is set in front of you by your Japanese hostess, and your only implement is a pair of chopsticks. You do not want to embarrass yourself or your hostess. You pick up your chopsticks and casually try to grasp the bite-sized pieces of food. You cannot make the chopsticks work effectively.

CASE STUDY REVIEW

How might you feel in a situation like this when you are hungry, helpless and you do not want to embarrass yourself? What do you do? First, think about your options. List three here.

1. ____________________

2. ____________________

3. ____________________

Then, ask yourself, "What are the pros and cons of each alternative?"

Option #1. *Pros* ____________________

Cons ____________________

Option #2. *Pros* ____________________

Cons ____________________

Option #3. *Pros* ____________________

Cons ____________________

What resources do you have at your disposal? ____________________

____

____

____

Let's review some options:

✓ Ask your hostess or host for assistance. Your hostess demonstrates, first showing you how to place the bottom chopstick in your hand and then the second chopstick above it. Then she shows you how to wiggle the top chopstick and pick up your food. You try it and find that you are very awkward an ineffective.

✓ You consider using your fingers but realize that is unacceptable.

✓ You ask for a fork, but your hostess has just moved from Japan and has no western-style eating instruments in the house.

✓ Your hostess has foreseen the potential problem and brings out a rubber band. She places it around the chopsticks, effectively holding them together. She then shows you how to manipulate the top chopstick to grasp the food. You eat the delicious meal, although you still feel somewhat uncoordinated. You let your embarrassment pass and enjoy the experience.

Consider your feelings about yourself and your hostess in this last option. Although you may feel somewhat embarrassed, you are grateful for your hostess' foresight in accommodating your needs.

Let's assume that the rubber band does not make it easier for you. You and your hostess can brainstorm together on how to solve this problem.

The desired outcome is to use two pieces of wood to pick up food. What other ways might you do it?

- Use one chopstick in each hand.
- Use one of the chopsticks to pierce each bite-sized piece of food.
- Put some sticky substance on the end that will hold the food.

Who knows, you may invent a better chopstick and millions of people around the world will be forever grateful!

You might try this exercise with your staff. Buy some inexpensive wooden chopsticks, pass them out at a staff meeting, and ask people how to modify those chopsticks so they are easier to use. Provide simple items such as paper clips, rubber bands, or tape for their use. As a final exam for yourself and your staff, get some jelly beans and practice transferring them from one plate or napkin to another. When you can do this easily, you will know that you can eat anything with chopsticks.

WHAT DOES THIS EXERCISE TEACH US?

During the exercise, you were ''chopstick impaired.'' (While this is a temporary disability, you probably experienced some of the same frustrations as a person with a more permanent disability during the first days on a new job.) You were unable to use the traditional tools of the job in the traditional way to accomplish the desired outcome. At first, you were clumsy and perhaps your production rate was not fast. With practice, you probably improved.

But suppose you lack coordination or you have missing fingers that would prevent you from ever using chopsticks competently in the traditional fashion. You may need to identify a modification. Perhaps the rubber band was sufficient. If not, you may need to redesign the chopsticks. You may need to use a different instrument such as a fork.

Remember how you and your hostess together determined the best way for you to enjoy your meal? The same principle applies to determining reasonable accommodation. Focus on the outcome rather than the modification. You and your employee with the disability need to jointly identify an accommodation. The ADA does not require the most expensive modification, only one that will overcome the limitations of the disability.

As a successful supervisor, you will often tap the creativity of those in your work group. This is the basis for Total Quality Improvement and work teams that continuously seek improved methods of accomplishing a task. Reasonable accommodation requires the same process in a different situation.

Similar exercises for another staff meeting:

- How many uses can you come up with for a paperclip?

- You are on your way to an important meeting and the heel on your shoe comes off; how would you fix it when you don't have time to stop at a shoe repair store?

Using exercises such as this every now and then in a workgroup can recharge people's creative batteries and get them thinking in nontraditional, yet effective ways. If this idea intrigues you, consider getting Roger von Oech's *Creative Whack Pack,* a deck of 64 cards that suggest new and innovative ways to look at problems.

DOCUMENTING ACCOMMODATION EFFORTS

While not required by the ADA, it is important to document the accommodation process and the accommodations that you provide. Why? It will be useful if . . .

- Additional workers need similar accommodations in the future.
- An employee ever challenges decisions to not provide additional accommodations.

Include in your documentation:

☐ The discussions that you have with the employee. (You *are* involving the person in the decision-making process, aren't you?)

☐ The cost of various accommodations you discuss (you are not required to provide the most expensive accommodation, only one that will make the employee productive). Document why you chose the accommodation you did.

☐ Alternative funding sources you identify (vocational rehabilitation agencies, accommodations the employee already owns, etc.).

☐ Time lines on accommodations which require time away from the job.

Don't mislead the employee about making an accommodation if you are not sure it is feasible.

Put your decisions in memo form to the employee so there are no misunderstandings.

DOCUMENTING ACCOMMODATION EFFORTS (continued)

Is permitting excessive absences a form of accommodation?

In a recent ruling (see Other Resources, page 117), the U.S. District Court for the District of Columbia found that regular attendance is an essential function of the job and an employee is not otherwise qualified to perform the job when that essential function cannot be met. This case is significant, because, although it was based on the Rehabilitation Act of 1973, it *may* be a forerunner of decisions concerning reasonable accommodation under the ADA.

The process of determining accommodations underscores the importance of having a good job description and outlining attendance responsibilities as an essential function.

When does accommodation become ''unreasonable'' rather than ''reasonable''?

The most ''reasonable'' accommodations may involve the purchase of equipment or modification of a work station. More difficulty arises when an employee with a progressive medical condition, such as severe arthritis or AIDS, needs more and more assistance or longer periods of time off for medical treatment.

Some ideas:

- Make sure that the employee understands the requirement to perform the essential functions of the job, including attendance requirements.

- Document discussions you and the employee have had about accommodations.

- If absences become burdensome, look at the possibility of switching to part-time work. Also consider allowing the employee to work at home or telecommute, with occasional time in the office. With modems and fax machines becoming more common, this may be reasonable.

ACCOMMODATING CURRENT EMPLOYEES WHO BECOME DISABLED

Anyone can become disabled at any time, either on or off the job. Auto accidents, sports-related injuries, or just growing older provide opportunities for people to become disabled during their working years. As people work longer, more will become disabled and qualify for protection under the ADA. Most people who will be protected under the ADA are not new, but present employees.

Why should you accommodate current employees?

- Your organization has spent time, energy, and money to develop employees into productive workers.
- Recruiting, hiring, and training new people is expensive.
- Accommodating present employees who become disabled is time and cost effective.

What can you do as a supervisor when an employee becomes disabled? Here are some steps to take to increase the chances that an employee will return to productivity quickly.

1. Review your organization's return to work policies with the HR department.
2. Let the newly disabled employee know of your support
    - If appropriate, send flowers.
    - It is always encouraging to say, "We miss you. What can we do to help you?"
    - Keep in touch regularly to enhance the person's interest in the job and co-workers.
3. Even if the person is not totally able to return to work, consider telecommuting if the job can be adapted to it. Provide equipment such as a computer, modem, or fax so the person can be productive according to physical stamina.
4. Consider having the person return part-time.

ACCOMMODATING CURRENT EMPLOYEES WHO BECOME DISABLED (continued)

Your chances for successful return are greatly increased if your organization has an early return-to-work policy and program.

Early return-to-work programs encourage and enable injured or disabled employees to return to work under medical supervision before they are fully recuperated. Organizations often identify light duty positions or provide for a period of part-time work progressing toward full-time, which capitalizes on a person's skills without demanding full physical functioning. They value retaining and retraining present employees rather than replacing them.

The ADA does not mandate an early return-to-work policy. However, as a supervisor, depending on your ADA philosophy, you may be reactive or proactive in helping a valued employee get back on the job as soon as medically feasible.

When a person is able to return, either full- or part-time, review the job description to determine the essential functions and talk with the employee about which of those functions can be done without accommodation. Identify duties that will require accommodation, and ask the employee if he or she knows which accommodations are needed. If not, ask if the person is working with an occupational therapist or a vocational rehabilitation specialist. If so, with the employee's permission, involve the rehabilitation professional in performing a job analysis to determine appropriate accommodations. Then make accommodations, either by restructuring the job in-house or providing accommodations from outside vendors or resources. Do not forget to let your accounting department know about tax credits.

Put accommodations in place and welcome your employee back to the job and allow for a period of readjustment.

Example of Successful Accommodation

An electronics manufacturing plant brought back an employee who lost an arm in a sports accident. When he was ready to return to work, the company made a short video tape of his job to show his doctor what the job required. The company brought an occupational therapist to the job site to recommend accommodations. The company made a sling to hold the employee's drill and had an outside manufacturer create some special tools and a stool. With a few accommodations, they retained the services of a valued employee.

Attitude Checkpoint

Let's see how our supervisor friends might react to this chapter.

Tammy Traditional might say, ''There's too much change, too many accommodations that might impact the way I do my business. I liked it better when things didn't change so much and I could do things the way I always have.''

Mark Middle-of-the-Road might respond, ''Well, the work regulations are changing, and I guess I'd better get used to helping employees with disabilities by considering some modifications in the work environment.''

Andy Assertive might say, ''Helping determine employee accommodations is exciting, and offers new opportunities to everyone on my staff. I should find out more about how I can give people with disabilities an equal chance at employment.''

You say, ____

____

____

____

____

____

P A R T

V

ADA: Support Services and Management Application

SUPPORT SERVICES FOR SUCCESSFUL SUPERVISORS

Because the ADA may present new challenges and opportunities, you may feel that there is no place to turn with questions. This section will help you recognize where you can get answers, both within your organization and outside.

Support Within the Organization

While supervisors will have primary responsibility for setting a tone of acceptance and working effectively with people with disabilities within their area, others in the organization must set policies related to ADA compliance and support your efforts.

Top management should, by this time, be well aware of ADA compliance requirements and be committed to complying. They may have developed policies, perhaps in conjunction with an attorney.

The human resources department should have revised employment procedures and communicated revisions to all staff.

Many companies have set up an ADA Task Force, comprised of representatives from various parts of the organization, including perhaps an attorney, safety personnel, a human resources representative, the facilities manager, and others. Progressive organizations have included present employees with disabilities to advise them on matters of policy, access, and reasonable accommodation.

Some human resource managers have established support groups with their peers from different companies. They meet occasionally to update each other on ADA news, brainstorm ideas, and solve problems.

Even if you cannot be part of a support group with outside organizations, you might set up an internal ADA group, separate from the official ADA Task Force, among supervisors. Even an informal lunchtime meeting with other supervisors could be beneficial. Be sure to share success stories.

In some organizations, people with disabilities have created support groups of their own. They also have made themselves available to managers and supervisors to offer assistance in training, reviewing essential functions and assisting new employees with disabilities become successful in the organization.

OUTSIDE SUPPORT

Disability Organizations

Every state has a vocational rehabilitation agency supported by state and federal taxes. Some states have two agencies, one specializing in working with people who are blind. These agencies assist people with disabilities to become employed or maintain their employment if they become disabled. They are invaluable sources of information, as well as recruiting resources for qualified, trained people who are looking for employment. Look in the telephone directory under Vocational Rehabilitation or Commission (or Services) for the Blind in the state agencies section.

Every community has organizations that offer services to people with disabilities as well as employers. Since the passage of the ADA, many have broadened their services to include employer education. Check your telephone directory under Social Service or Rehabilitation, then look for the name of a specific disability. A phone call will usually bring either informational pamphlets or a speaker. Use the information in your community to increase your awareness.

Some agencies that serve people who are blind also have technology centers where you can view the latest equipment such as braille and speech output computers. You are welcome to visit to get an idea of how a person who is blind can access computers.

Vocational rehabilitation agencies sometimes offer job analysis and assistance in determining reasonable accommodation, especially if one of their clients is looking for a job in your area.

Private rehabilitation agencies also provide training and placement support for people with disabilities.

Using the phone book, list two rehabilitation agencies in your area.

1. ______________________________

2. ______________________________

All of the agencies should be knowledgeable about technical assistance programs and tax credits you can use to offset the possible additional costs of hiring a qualified individual with a disability.

Supported Employment Programs

''Supported employment'' is a term you may not know. It refers to employing people who may be severely disabled and traditionally not in the workforce. Under supported employment, a person who is developmentally disabled, mentally ill, or who has had a traumatic brain injury works with a vocational rehabilitation agency to identify skills and interests, much the same process as other clients of VR agencies. An employment specialist works with an employer to identify an appropriate job for the person. Then, when the person has begun working, the ''job coach'' provided by the agency will provide on-the-job training and follow-along support for the person, perhaps for several months. The job coach will assure good quality and will relieve the supervisor of the intense training the person may need, especially early in employment. Job coaches can also train co-workers about how to work effectively with the employee with the disability. Generally, the job coach ''fades'' gradually as the person becomes more proficient and the ''natural support'' of co-workers takes over.

Some companies have ''enclaves,'' where several employees with disabilities are hired, usually in one area doing the same type of work, ''coached'' by one job coach who oversees and provides training to the group, gradually fading as employees learn and produce more.

While supported employment originally involved only people with developmental disabilities, companies are hiring those with other impairments. In a recent study involving supported employment for people with long-term mental illness, researchers found the following:

- Most employers who have hired workers with psychiatric disabilities found these workers had no problem integrating into the workforce.
- If forced to reduce staff, over 80 percent of employers said they would not automatically fire a supported-employment worker.
- Eighty-four percent said they would hire another individual with mental illness.

The benefit of supported employment for you as a supervisor is that you hire a person with a disability and have support for training both the employee and co-workers. The job coach can make it easy for you.

To find out more about supported employment possibilities for your company, contact your state vocational rehabilitation agency or the county mental health or developmental disabilities agency.

OUTSIDE SUPPORT (continued)

High Schools

Your local high school may have a placement program for its graduates who have disabilities. You can meet with a "transition coordinator" who can identify students with skills you need in your workforce. Quite often, these students need unpaid work experience, and you may serve as a site for them. In this case, you would be under no obligation to hire, but may provide feedback about the person's skills and work habits, encouraging the person to develop further before entering the workforce full-time.

High schools and some rehabilitation agencies sometimes have summer work experience programs for students with disabilities. If you traditionally hire extra help in the summer, consider contacting these organizations to find capable young people who need a start to their careers.

Graduates of programs for students with disabilities need opportunities for that important first job. You can talk with a rehabilitation specialist or transition coordinator about the skills these students have and the type of work for which they are most suited.

Community Colleges and Universities

You need a well-trained workforce. Students graduating from technical schools, colleges, and universities in your area may have the latest knowledge in your field. Most schools have a Disabled Student Services Office. These offices have usually developed a strong relationship with students with disabilities throughout their academic career. They also know what accommodations have worked for them.

You can approach one of these offices, identify the jobs for which you have openings, and request referrals of qualified applicants. You can also offer to serve as an internship site for a student who needs work experience. This offers you the opportunity to work with a student with a disability without committing to hire the person permanently. Often, students with disabilities will be clients of the vocational rehabilitation system, with the support of vocational counselors and rehabilitation technology specialists who can help determine reasonable accommodations.

One of the most positive steps you can take to effectively implement the ADA is to establish an on-going relationship with organizations which are knowledgeable about the capabilities of people with disabilities and work on their behalf. They will also work on your behalf to assist you in finding and successfully employing qualified individuals with disabilities.

What resources have you used in the past to get information about the ADA or people with disabilities? ____________________

____

Have you established a file of ADA materials in your work area that you and your workgroup members can use?

Yes____ No____ (If no, please consider doing so.)

Attitude Checkpoint

What might our three supervisors do to determine what support services are available to them for assisting employees with disabilities?

Tammy Traditional might say she looked in the phone book and identified one of the listed organizations.

Maria Middle-of-the-Road might say she called several organizations and asked them to send her literature for future reference.

Andy Assertive might say he made appointments with a cross-section of agencies providing a variety of services to people with disabilities to come and describe their services. He included representatives from the human resources and some of his staff in the meeting so they could all learn about the many support options.

You might say: ____________________

____

____

____

____

A SUCCESSFUL APPLICATION OF ADA

Let's put everything together and see how you might use this information to successfully supervise in the ADA era.

CASE STUDY #3

Chan is an accounting supervisor in a high-tech firm. The department is expanding, and he has an opening for an accounting clerk. He determines the essential needs of the job to be: calculating, posting, and verifying duties to obtain financial data for use in maintaining accounting records. Essential functions are:

✓ compiling and sorting documents such as invoices and checks to substantiate business transactions;

✓ verifying and posting details of business transactions, such as funds received and disbursed, and totaling accounts;

✓ computing and recording charges, refunds, costs of damaged goods, freight charges;

✓ preparing vouchers, invoices, checks, and other records using the computer

Chan determines that marginal functions of the job are:

✓ keeping track of accounting office supplies and reordering when necessary

✓ distributing accounting reports to other offices around the company

Chan likes to give young people an opportunity and he wants someone who has had recent training in entry-level accounting work. He has heard about the ADA and would like to find a qualified person with a disability to fill the job.

If you were Chan, how would you proceed? ____________________________

____

____

____

Where might you find someone with the skills you need? ______________________

____

____

Chan contacts the Office for Disabled Students at his local community college. He provides a copy of the job description to Flavia, the person who helps disabled students find work. Flavia knows that Kim will graduate in a few weeks with an associate's degree in accounting. She is starting to look for an entry-level job in her area and has asked Flavia to pass along job announcements to her. Flavia gives the announcement to Kim, who contacts Chan at the company. They agree to meet in Chan's office. Kim asks Chan if his office is accessible, since she is a wheelchair user. Chan assures her that the office has been assessed and should be OK.

Kim arrives at the appointed time and meets Chan. She gives him her resume, which shows good grades and some prior office work experience. Chan reviews the job description with her, asking her whether she can perform the essential functions he has outlined. She assures him she can, offering examples from her coursework and experience. Although Chan is curious about the effect her disability might have on her work, he sticks to describing the job and asking about her ability to perform essential functions.

Kim asks to see the office in which the job is located. They go into the area and discover that the partitions that make the cubicles are too close to the outside wall for her to pass. They go around another way and find that the opening of the cubicle is also too narrow for her wheelchair. They look at another office that is a little larger. They discover that the computer desk is too low for her wheelchair to fit under. Kim asks Chan how much time is spent using the computer, explaining that, because of weakness in her hands, she can be more productive using a different style keyboard.

Kim also points out to Chan that she would have difficulty performing the marginal functions listed on the job description. The accounting office supplies are in cabinets that are above her reach in the storeroom. In addition, because of the age and configuration of the building, not all offices are accessible to her, making delivery of reports difficult.

CASE STUDY #3 (continued)

They discuss these limitations and agree that either the supplies could be moved to lower cabinets or this job duty could be assigned to someone else. In exchange, Kim could take on another duty. Also, they brainstormed ways to deliver the reports, and Chan finally admitted that he had been considering offering the reports through e-mail to the other offices but had just not gotten around to setting that up.

Chan offers Kim the job, contingent upon passing the company-required drug screening and a physical exam required of all applicants to whom a job has been offered. Kim accepts, and invites Chan to the community college to see the equipment she has been using. She also invites Chan to meet her counselor from the Vocational Rehabilitation Division, who may be able to help defray expenses involved in modifying the job.

Kim passes the drug screen, and the results of the physical exam show that Kim is in good health. The doctor reviewed the job description outlining essential functions and finds no reason why Kim should not be able to perform those functions.

Chan consults the company's facility manager to request that the movable partitions be configured to allow Kim easy access to her office. The ladies room, the lunchroom, the drinking fountain, and other areas are accessible. He also writes up a performance expectation list and arranges for someone else to order supplies.

Chan and Kim meet with the vocational rehabilitation counselor. Chan is delighted to find that the plan for helping Kim become employed contains funding for some equipment, so costs to the company will be minimal, primarily those in making the office more accessible. The counselor also explains currently available tax credits to Chan, and he promises to pass the information along to the company accountant. The counselor orders the adapted computer keyboard for Kim and arranges to have it delivered to Chan's company.

At the next department meeting, Chan reviews ADA information with his workgroup, as well as indicating that a new employee has been hired to fill the accounting clerk position. He outlines Kim's experience and indicates that she will graduate from the community college next week. He also talks about his philosophy of hiring and supervising people with disabilities and indicates that Kim uses a wheelchair. He describes the changes that have been made in the work area to permit her wheelchair to pass unimpeded. He reminds the group that Kim was hired on the basis of her experience, her recent training, and her potential to be a productive member of the department.

He said he hoped people would make her feel welcome. He assigned each member of the workgroup a topic for her orientation as he had done in the past for other new employees. Some members of the group ask what they have to do special for Kim, and he replies, "She is independent and capable. She may need to have something brought down from high shelves, but otherwise should need no assistance." Someone asks the cause of her disability, and Chan says, "I don't know, and her medical information is confidential, just as yours would be."

Kim's special keyboard arrives and Chan installs it. He checks to ensure that all access requirements have been completed, then walks to the door Monday morning. "Welcome, Kim. We're glad you're here."

CASE STUDY REVIEW

Here's an example of a successful process of hiring a qualified person with a disability, involving the community college and vocational rehabilitation agency, working with the candidate to determine what modifications would maximize her potential, getting financial assistance with the costs of accommodation, and dealing with co-worker concerns.

This is a win-win situation. You can duplicate this experience, perhaps not in the details, but in the results.

What would you need to do to replicate this success? ____________________

____

____

YOUR NEW ACTION PLAN

All the information in this book will be wasted if you do not use it—along with what you have learned about yourself—to plan for meeting the opportunities you have to benefit from workers with disabilities.

Let's set some goals for yourself that will help you in these efforts.

Answer the following questions thoughtfully and in as much detail as will be useful to you.

Needs within yourself (how can I meet them?)

I Need . . .

I need to learn more about:

- the ADA ______________________________
- people with disabilities ______________________________
- communicating effectively with those I supervise ______________________________

How can I meet these needs?

- training (by whom?) ______________________________
- talking with others in my organization (who?) ______________________________
- taking a class (where?) ______________________________
- reading (what?) ______________________________

Things I need to discuss with my supervisor:

- ______________________________
- ______________________________

Things I need to find out from the organization's human resource department about our ADA implementation efforts:

- ______________________________
- ______________________________

The Organization Needs . . .

Needs I have identified within the organization related to complying with the ADA and involving people with disabilities more fully in our workforce . . .

____

____

Who can deal with them? ____

____

What impact can I have on seeing these needs met? ____________________

____

What Can I Do?

Within my department to create an atmosphere of acceptance of people with disabilities? ____

____

To be provided to my staff to assist them in welcoming people with disabilities as colleagues and co-workers? ______________________________

____

Regarding successfully supervising employees with disabilities and implementing the Americans with Disabilities Act, I commit to: ____________________

____

Timeline to meet these identified needs:

By ____________, I will ____

____

PART

VI

The Americans with Disabilities Act of 1990

ADA: AN OVERVIEW

Do you need to read this chapter?

Yes—if you turned to this first because you have had no exposure to information about the ADA or if you'd like a brief review before you look specifically at how the ADA affects your life as a supervisor. If your answers on the True/False test showed gaps in your knowledge, this is a good place to start.

No—if you are familiar with the definitions and basic premises of the ADA.

How the ADA Impacts Supervisors

The Americans with Disabilities Act was signed into law by President George Bush on July 26, 1990. Its purpose is to provide equal opportunities in all aspects of life for America's 43 million people with disabilities.

The ADA has five sections, called Titles. They cover the following:

Title I: Employment

Title II: Public Services

Title III: Public Accommodations

Title IV: Telecommunications

Title V: Miscellaneous

This book concentrates primarily on Title I. Realize that if you are a supervisor in a government organization, covered by Title II, you are also covered by Titles I and III.

ADA: AN OVERVIEW (continued)

History of the ADA

The ADA is one of a long line of laws designed to bring people with disabilities into the mainstream of American life.

- ► The Civil Rights Act of 1964 forbid discrimination based on race, religion, ethnicity, and sex. It did not include people with disabilities.

- ► The Rehabilitation Act of 1973 required Federal contractors to not discriminate against people with disabilities and to accommodate their needs on the job.

- ► Other laws have impacted transportation and housing for people with disabilities. No law provided all the rights and privileges of citizenship to America's disabled citizens. The ADA is meant to rectify that oversight.

There is an important distinction between the ADA, which is a ''nondiscrimination'' law, and other laws which require ''affirmative action.''

- ''Nondiscrimination'' means equal opportunity to apply for and work in jobs, and be considered for promotion along with other qualified people.

- ''Affirmative action'' means that an organization plans for and actively seeks candidates in protected classes.

The ADA has no recruiting requirements. It does require that organizations look first at a person's abilities rather than automatically excluding them on the basis of perceived inability resulting from a disability.

Organizations Covered by the ADA

Title I of the ADA, which prohibits discrimination in hiring, took effect for companies with 25 or more employees on July 26, 1992. It takes effect for companies of 15 or more employees on July 26, 1994. It covers all employers, including state and federal agencies, except private clubs and religious organizations.

Title I of the ADA covers all aspects of employment, including the following. These are just samples of some of the main areas in which you, as a supervisor, may be involved. More complete information is provided elsewhere in the book.

Employees Covered by the ADA

The ADA is a comprehensive law. If your organization is large enough to be covered, then all employees will be covered:

- CEO to the janitor (all job titles)
- current employees who already have a disability
- current employees who become disabled in the future
- applicants and newly hired employees
- those who associate with people with disabilities

Let's look at how the ADA affects these groups of applicants and employees.

Current Employees Who Are Disabled—Your organization may already have employees with disabilities. Some of the disabilities may be visible, such as someone who has a mobility impairment and uses a wheelchair or crutches to get around. You may have someone who is legally blind or is deaf, or someone with severe arthritis. Consider, however, that you may also have employees who are disabled but whose disabilities have never been recognized. For example, 10–15 percent of the working population is considered learning disabled. Someone who is an excellent assembly worker may have difficulty filling out a work order or completing statistical process control paperwork. Maybe you wonder why his or her production skills are so good but the paperwork skills are so bad. The individual may have a learning disability that affects the ability to complete paperwork accurately.

Someone may hide a visual loss for fear of dismissal should it become known. You may have someone who is HIV positive but has not told anyone in the organization for fear of being let go. You may have someone who has cancer but has not let anyone know.

All these current employees may be disabled under the ADA but for one reason or another have not let anyone know, probably for fear that they would be fired. Since the ADA, more people with disabilities are becoming aware of their rights and current employees may now have the courage to come to you and request accommodation. You need to be prepared for this possibility.

A note of caution: Do not assume that any performance problem you notice is disability-based. Do not try to diagnose a person's disability or second-guess the *cause* of the performance problem. Deal with the performance problem as you would with anyone else. The ADA only requires that you accommodate a *known* disability and it does not require that you become a medical doctor or psychologist to diagnose disability.

ADA: AND OVERVIEW (continued)

Current Employees Who Become Disabled—*Disability is only a heartbeat or footstep away for any of us.* Recognizing that, the ADA protects from discrimination any employee who may become disabled, either on the job or off.

Applicants and Newly Hired Employees

The ADA will encourage more people with disabilities than ever to enter the workforce for the first time, including . . .

- People who have been disabled all of their lives but have never before worked
- Those who have been employed as disabled workers but for a different organization.
- Young people with disabilities who have been provided services under Public Law 94-142 and the Individuals with Disabilities Education Act.

These young people may be different from others because their disabilities have been accommodated in the school setting, perhaps all of their educational life. They will expect accommodation as they move into the workforce. They will be more knowledgeable about their rights as disabled Americans than older workers who become disabled.

Associates of People with Disabilities

The ADA recognizes that discrimination exists against people who live with or associate with people with disabilities. A mother who has a son with cerebral palsy, for example, may be perceived by her employer as someone who may need extensive time off to care for him. Someone who volunteers in a hospice may be perceived as a potential person with a disability or at risk for becoming disabled. While the ADA does not require employers to accommodate those who associate with people with disabilities, it does require that we not discriminate against them in any aspect of employment.

PRE-HIRE FUNCTIONS COVERED BY THE ADA

Interviewing Rooms

Areas where you meet applicants must be accessible to people with physical disabilities, including those who use wheelchairs. In addition, major changes are required in the way most people assess applicants.

Questions

Interviewers may not ask questions about a person's perceived or actual disability. Questions can only investigate a person's ability to perform the "essential functions" of a job. This means that organizations should conduct a job analysis of each job and list the essential functions of the job prior to advertising any opening. As a supervisor, you may be asked to conduct such analysis, or at least approve the resulting job description. Job descriptions will be much more thorough than in the past (See Chapter 4).

Reasonable Accommodation

If a person indicates a need for reasonable accommodation during the application process, the company is required to provide it. A person who is deaf can request an interpreter be hired at company expense for the interview. If hired, the company also may be responsible for providing reasonable accommodations on the job, unless doing so would present an undue hardship for the company.

Testing

If employment tests are used, they must be relevant to the essential functions of the job and must be given in alternative formats for people who cannot test in the usual fashion.

PRE-HIRE FUNCTIONS COVERED BY THE ADA (continued)

Medical Exams

During the interview, no reference can be made to a person's disability. The ADA has specific requirements about when medical examinations may be done and the handling of the results. The ADA forbids medical examinations until after a conditional offer of employment has been made. An offer of employment can be made contingent upon a person passing a job-related physical exam.

Drug Testing

The ADA does not affect drug testing. If drug tests are required for all applicants, disabled applicants may also be required to take the drug test.

Confidentiality

The ADA requires a higher degree of confidentiality than you may be used to. Any results of medical tests and any information about a person's disability must be kept in a separate locked location with limited access.

Your human resource department should be aware of these changes, and hopefully, has established policies and guidelines that you can use. You will want to check with your human resources department for guidance before you interview. Any mistake you make could be costly and legally troubling for you and your organization.

QUIZ

Let's see how well you can apply the basics of ADA now.

1. A person who is deaf comes to your employment office to apply for a file clerk job. She hands the receptionist a note indicating her interest, along with a copy of her resume indicating previous experience as a file clerk in another city. What should the receptionist do?

   ___

   ___

2. You set up an interview with the person described in question 1. Your first question to her is, "So, have you always been deaf?" Is that a legal question under the ADA? Explain why or why not.

   ___

   ___

3. You ask the applicant to take a test on alphabetical and numerical filing. Is this appropriate under the ADA? Explain why or why not.

   ___

   ___

4. You say to the candidate, "We require all applicants to take a physical exam. Please stop by the receptionist's desk and set up an appointment." Is that proper procedure, according to the ADA? Explain why or why not.

   ___

   ___

How well did you do? See answers in Appendix, page 118. If you need more specific information on these issues, consult the *Americans with Disabilities* described in the bibliography.

POST-HIRE RESPONSIBILITIES

Once a person with a disability has been hired and has indicated a need for reasonable accommodation, it is incumbent upon the organization to provide accommodations, in consultation with the person with a disability.

While accommodation must be provided if it does not present an ''undue hardship,'' it does not have to be the most expensive accommodation. It must, however, enable the person to overcome the disability in order to effectively and productively perform the essential functions of the job.

Additional Management Considerations

Supervision

Supervising a person with a disability should not be difficult. People with disabilities come in all shapes, sizes, colors, communication styles, and personalities, just like employees without disabilities. If you are faced with a supervisory situation in which you are uncertain about how to act or what to do, the rule of thumb is, **Use Courtesy, Communication and Common Sense.**

Training

Any training you provide to your employees must be available to people with disabilities. The training location must be accessible, and you may need to adapt training materials to a format which provides the best opportunity for learning, despite a person's disability, such as limited vision or hearing or a learning disability.

It is important that people with disabilities have the opportunity to attend training away from the office. If a training session is out of town or at a site away from the accessible worksite, you must ensure that it is accessible to all participants. Training related events such as meals, to which all trainees must go, shall be accessible so that a person with a disability can be included. We all know that a lot of learning takes place over dinner and at the social events people attend together. The disabled person has a right to attend *all* events related to the training.

Promotion

Underemployment of people with disabilities is almost as great a problem as unemployment. Supervisors may mistakenly assume that a person with a disability is happy with an entry level job and has no aspirations beyond that. The ADA asks you to recognize a person's ambitions and offer the same opportunities for career planning and advancement as you would any employee.

If a promotion requires new forms of accommodation to allow the people with disabilities to be fully productive, you and the disabled employee will work together to determine which accommodation will meet the needs. This will give you both a chance to identify work-related issues before they become problems.

Benefits

The ADA specifically prohibits employers from discriminating against employees with disabilities in any form of compensation, benefit or condition of employment. Ask your HR office for the latest information about how the ADA affects compensation and benefit plans.

As a supervisor, you may have authority over some benefits—especially "perks" that your employees earn or negotiate. Do not assume that a person with a disability would not, for example, want a health club membership just because the person uses a wheelchair. Company-run health clubs must be accessible to and useable by people with disabilities, and many people with disabilities use them for swimming, weight lifting—the same activities that nondisabled people enjoy.

Attitude Checkpoint

Let's look at how our three supervisors might react to the material in this chapter.

Tom Traditional might quickly review an ADA pamphlet that crossed his desk and complain about more laws and government interference in the way companies do business. When he has a job opening, he may pull out an old position description and hope it's OK. If a person with a disability were to apply and come in for an interview, he might ask, ''So, why do you want to work, anyway? Don't you get government benefits so you don't have to work?''

Maria Middle-of-the-Road might attend a half-day company-sponsored ADA training session. She'd key in on those ''amazing'' people with disabilities like Helen Keller. She might update a job description when she had a vacancy, and may read a list of interview questions which are no longer allowable under the ADA. If a person with a disability applied for an opening, she might consider someone who looked particularly outstanding, but would hire the person hesitantly. If that person didn't work out, she'd probably say, ''Well, I tried one person with a disability, but don't ask me to try another.''

Andy Assertive would probably bring in a qualified ADA trainer and involve present employees who have disabilities in providing sensitivity training to himself and others on the staff. He would review department plans and all position descriptions, making sure that he has identified essential functions. He might send job announcements to Disabled Student Service Offices at local community colleges, universities and vocational schools. He would make sure that his application process, including the room where interviews are held, is accessible and comfortable for all candidates. If a person with a disability applied for a job, Andy might ask during the interview, ''One of the essential functions of this job is to access information for our customers from a database. I understand you have computer experience. Can you tell me how you access information without being able to see the computer screen?''

You, the successful supervisor, might: ______________________________

____

____

____

APPENDIX

ADA RESOURCES

There is no lack of information about the ADA and people with disabilities. The following are just a few of the sources. Contact Creative Compliance Management for other possibilities.

Job Accommodation Network

The Job Accommodation Network, commonly called JAN, is a service of the President's Committee on Employment of People with Disabilities. By calling a toll-free number (800-526-7234 or 800-ADA-WORK), you will meet a Human Factors Consultant. You tell the person about the limitations of a person with a disability and the type of job involved. The consultant suggests accommodations that may make it possible for the person with a disability to be successful in that job. JAN does not sell adaptive equipment, but lets you know what has worked elsewhere. In exchange, JAN would like to know your results.

Regional Disability and Business Accommodation Centers

Each of the ten Federal regions has a Regional Disability and Business Accommodation Center set up by the National Institute on Disability and Rehabilitation Research. These offices provide free telephone assistance as well as a supply of government publications on the ADA. If the following numbers are incorrect, call (800) 949-4232 (voice or TDD) for additional information.

Region I: Connecticut, Maine, Massachusetts, New Hampshire, Rhode Island, Vermont:

New England Disability and Business	(207) 874-6535 (voice/TDD*)
Technical Assistance Center	(207) 874-6529 (fax)
145 Newbury Street;	(800) 949-4232 (voice/TDD)
Portland, ME 04101	

Region II: New York, New Jersey, Puerto Rico, Virgin Islands

Northeast Disability and Business	(609) 392-4004 (voice)
Technical Assistance Center	(609) 392-7004 (TDD)
354 South Broad Street;	(800) 487-2805 (voice)
Trenton, NJ 08608	(800) 676-2831 (TDD)

ADA RESOURCES (continued)

Region III: Delaware, District of Columbia, Maryland, Pennsylvania, Virginia, West Virginia

Mid-Atlantic Disability and Business	(703) 525-3268 (voice/TDD)
Technical Assistance Center	
2111 Wilson Boulevard, Suite 400;	
Arlington, VA 22201	

Region IV: Alabama, Florida, Georgia, Kentucky, Mississippi, North Carolina, South Carolina, Tennessee

Southeast Disability and Business	(404) 888-0022 (voice)
Technical Assistance Center	(404) 888-9098 (TDD)
1776 Peachtree Road, Suite 310 North;	(404) 888-9091 (fax)
Atlanta, GA 30309	

Region V: Illinois, Indiana, Michigan, Minnesota, Ohio, Wisconsin

Great Lakes Disability and Business	(312) 413-7756 (voice)
Technical Assistance Center (M/C 627)	(312) 413-0453 (TDD)
1640 West Roosevelt Road;	(800) 729-8275 (voice/TDD)
Chicago, IL 60608	(312) 413-1326 (fax)

Region VI: Arkansas, Louisiana, New Mexico, Oklahoma, Texas

Southwest Disability and Business	(713) 520-0232 (voice)
Technical Assistance Center	(713) 520-5136 (TDD)
2323 S. Shepherd, Suite 1000;	(800) 949-4ADA (voice/TDD)
Houston, TX 77019	

Region VII: Iowa, Kansas, Nebraska, Missouri

Great Plains Disability and Business	(314) 882-3807 (voice/TDD)
Technical Assistance Center	
University of Missouri at Columbia;	
401 E. Locust St.;	
Columbia, MO 65201	

Region VIII: Colorado, Montana, North Dakota, South Dakota, Utah, Wyoming

Rocky Mountain Disability and
Business Technical Assistance Center
3630 Sinton Road, Suite 103;
Colorado Springs, CO 80907-5072

(719) 444-0252
(800) 735-4ADA (voice/TDD)
(719) 444-0269 (fax)

Region IX: Arizona, California, Hawaii, Nevada, Pacific Basin

Pacific Disability and Business
Technical Assistance Center
440 Grand Avenue, Suite 500;
Oakland, CA 94610

(510) 465-7884 (voice)
(510) 465-3172 (TDD)

Region X: Alaska, Idaho, Oregon, Washington

Northwest Disability and Business
Technical Assistance Center
P.O. Box 9046;
Olympia, WA 98507-9046

(800) HELP-ADA (voice/TDD)
(206) 438-4014 (fax)

Other Resources

Epilepsy Information Line: (800) 322-1000

U.S. District Court for the District of Columbia case:
Carr v. Barr, 59, Empl. Prac. Dec. (CCH) Para. 41, 651; June 23, 1992.

ANSWERS TO EXERCISES

Match Game Answers (from page 6)

How well did you match up the following well-known people and their disabilities?

CONTRIBUTOR	DISABILITY
Cher	Dyslexia
Chris Burke	Down's syndrome
Bruce Jenner	Learning disability
James Brady	Head injury
Stephen Hawking	Amyotrophic lateral sclerosis
Ray Charles	Blind
Ann Jillian	Cancer
Whoopi Goldberg	Learning Disability
Itzhak Perlman	Polio
Marlee Matlin	Deaf
President John F. Kennedy	Back problems
Mary Tyler Moore	Diabetes
Danny Glover	Epilepsy
Sammy Davis, Jr.	Visual impairment
Annette Funicello	Multiple sclerosis
Governor George Wallace	Paraplegia
President Franklin Roosevelt	Polio
Margaux Hemingway	Epilepsy
Virginia Woolf	Mental illness
Representative Barbara Jordan	Multiple sclerosis
Patricia Neal	Stroke

Quiz Answers (from page 107)

1. Your receptionist should have received training on the ADA and know that she could write a note back to the interested person offering to set up an appointment. The receptionist should ask if the applicant needs an interpreter, and, if so, does she have a preference. The receptionist should offer to send a confirmation note when an interpreter has been scheduled, then thank the person for her interest. Both parties should be clear on the timing and responsibilities of the next steps.
2. *No!* You cannot ask a question about a person's disability during the interview. You need to concentrate on the skills the person brings to the job.
3. *Yes!* If the test actually tests the skills required on the job, it may be considered "job related" and acceptable under the ADA.
4. *No!* You must offer the person a job, making the offer contingent on successfully passing the physical exam, not the other way around. This is a major change under the ADA.

True or False Quiz Answers (from page xii)

1. **TRUE** The intent of ADA is to protect all ''qualified individuals with disabilities.'' The use of ''Americans'' in the title is not restrictive. The ADA reflects a national sense of fairness and equality that recognizes the contributions of all individuals.

2. **TRUE** The ADA does not invalidate or limit any Federal, state or local law that provides greater or equivalent protection to individuals with disabilities. An individual may pursue a claim under all applicable laws.

3. **FALSE** The definition of a disability is divided into three parts. A physical or mental impairment that substantially limits one or more major life activities; a record of such an impairment; or being regarded as having such an impairment. Mitigating measures such as medicines, or assistive or prosthetic devices do not negate the existence of an impairment.

4. **FALSE** Economic, cultural, or environmental factors such as poverty or an inadequate education are not impairments even if they are disadvantages.

5. **TRUE** Physical characteristics that are not the result of a physiological disorder are not impairments. Similarly, personality traits that are not symptoms of a mental or psychological disorder such as poor judgement do not qualify as an impairment.

6. **FALSE** Many impairments do not affect ''major life activities.'' An impairment may be disabling for one individual but not for others. The ''effect'' of an impairment is critical and must be determined on a case by case consideration.

7. **FALSE** Myths, fears and stereotypes can substantially limit a persons ability to work. Negative reactions of others cannot be used as the basis for an employment decision.

8. **FALSE** The determination of whether an individual with a disability is qualified should be based on capabilities at the time of the employment decision. Speculation about future abilities, health conditions, or possible adverse changes in insurance risks, could constitute discrimination.

ANSWERS TO EXERCISES (continued)

9. **TRUE** One factor in determining essential functions is the number of other employees available to perform that job function. If a limited number of employees are available for the volume of work required, a function may be essential based on staff size. A similar situation might occur with a larger work force when work flow cycles of heavy demand require intense effort followed by slow periods.

10. **FALSE** Employers are not required to develop or maintain job descriptions. Written job descriptions, the employer's judgement, collective bargaining agreements, and past employees work experience are among the relevant evidence to be considered in determining essential job functions.

11. **FALSE** Employers are not required to lower production standards. However, if an employer intentionally selects a level of production to exclude individuals with disabilities, the employer may have to demonstrate legitimate, nondiscriminatory reasons for that production standard.

12. **TRUE** The ADA is intended to enable qualified individuals with disabilities to compete in the work force with or without reasonable accommodation. An accommodation is any change that enables an individual with a disability to enjoy equal employment opportunities including the application process.

13. **TRUE** Employers are required to provide equal access to employee benefits which may include health insurance. The ADA does not affect pre-existing conditions clauses that may have an adverse affect on some employees so long as the clauses are not used as a subterfuge to evade the purpose of the law.

14. **TRUE** Reasonable accommodations are intended to remove or alleviate employment barriers. Reassignment to a vacant position may be reasonable if an accommodation within the individuals current position would pose an undue hardship. The reassignment may not be used to limit, segregate or otherwise discriminate. It should be an equivalent position. Reassignment is not available to new applicants.

15. **FALSE** Accommodations include areas that must be accessible for work as well as non-work areas used by all employees. Lunch rooms, training areas and restrooms may be subject to modifications to achieve reasonable accommodations.

16. **FALSE** Rescheduling a job by altering when an essential function is performed may be a reasonable accommodation when a disability precludes performance at a customary hour.

17. **TRUE** Any significant expense or difficulty that would fundamentally alter the operation of a business may be an "undue hardship." However, if an alternative accommodation would not create an undue hardship, the employer would be required to provide that reasonable accommodation.

18. **TRUE** An employer may refuse to hire an otherwise qualified individual with a disability who poses a direct threat to himself or others if no accommodation exists that would eliminate or reduce the risk. An employer may not deny employment based on a slightly increased risk. All considerations must be made on a case by case basis.

19. **FALSE** Drug testing is not considered a medical examination. The ADA neither encourages nor prohibits testing for illegal use of drugs.

20. **FALSE** It is unlawful to discriminate against any qualified individual because that person is known to have an association with an individual who is disabled. This protection is not limited to a familial relationship.

21. **FALSE** Any accommodation is sufficient as long as it meets the job-related needs of the individual. The employer should consider all factors, including employee preference, effectiveness and cost when making a decision.

22. **FALSE** An employer cannot be expected to accommodate a disability when there is no knowledge of its existence. It is the responsibility of the individual with a disability to request an accommodation if needed.

23. **FALSE** The ADA is not an affirmative action program. It does not require preferences favoring individuals with disabilities over other applicants. The ADA requires employers to remove employment barriers to ensure equal employment opportunities.

24. **TRUE** If an accommodation is necessary, and refused, the individual may not be able to perform the essential functions of the job and would no longer be qualified.

25. **FALSE** Medical examinations and inquiries as to the nature or severity of a disability are prohibited. However, an employer may ask applicants to demonstrate how they would perform job-related functions with or without a reasonable accommodation.

ANSWER TO EXERCISES (continued)

26. TRUE Job-related dexterity test may be given to all similarly situated applicants at any point in the application or employment process. Such test are not considered medical examinations.

27. TRUE A job-related medical examination may be required after making an offer of employment. Employment may be based on the results of the examination provided all entering employees in the same job category are subject to such an examination.

28. FALSE Medical examinations may be required to determine fitness for duty. The collection of this information should be on separate forms and treated as confidential medical records.

29. TRUE The individual with a disability could volunteer to pay for a part or all of the cost of an accommodation found to be an undue hardship. Alternative sources of funding such as a qualified tax credit or a grant might also be used to reduce cost to an acceptable level.

30. TRUE The spirit of ADA is intended to provide individuals with disabilities access to the mainstream of American life. While legal remedies are available, common sense and constructive attitudes will result in substantial benefits to all parties.

Revised 2/92

BIBLIOGRAPHY

Dickson, Mary B. and Michael Mobley. *The Americans with Disabilities Act: Impact on Training.* American Society for Training and Development, 1992 (703/683-8129, $10).

Americans with Disabilities Act Technical Assistance Manual. Prepared jointly by the Equal Employment Opportunity Commission and the Justice Department. Basic, readable resource which every supervisor should have. Available for $25 from the closest U.S. Government Printing Office Bookstore.

Bolles, Richard Nelson. *Job-Hunting Tips for the So-Called Handicapped or People Who Have Disabilities.* Berkeley, CA: Ten Speed Press, 1991. $4.95. Why would I recommend this book? Because it contains the answers to many of your fears (as a supervisor) about hiring people with disabilities and it points out the issues that disabled job-seekers face. Pleasant and informative.

Dickson, Mary, B. and Michael Mobley. *The Americans with Disabilities Act: Techniques for Accommodation.* Alexandria, VA: American Society for Training and Development, 1992. Suggestions for accommodating employees with disabilities in training (703/683-8129, $10).

DuPont Company. *Equal to the Task II: 1990 DuPont Survey of Employment of People with Disabilities.* Write DuPont, Attn: G51932, P.O. Box 90029, Wilmington, DE 19880-0029, or call (800) 527-2601. A free booklet showing the results of DuPont's latest survey and vignettes of successful employees with disabilities.

Frierson, James G. *Employer's Guide to The Americans with Disabilities Act* was published in 1992 by BNA Books, 1250 23rd St NW, Washington, DC 20037-1165, (800) 372-1033 for $45. For each specific disability, sections include The Problem, Treatment, Accommodations, and Sources of Information.

Fritz, G. and N. Smith. *The Hearing Impaired Employee: An Untapped Resource.* San Diego: College-Hill Press, 1985.

Jamieson, David and Julie O'Mara. *Managing Workforce 2000: Gaining the Diversity Advantage.* San Francisco: Jossey-Bass Publishers, 1991. Looks at hiring and supervising people with disabilities. Provides good examples.

Koglin, Oz, Hopkins. "Looking into Hell: Progress in Brain Research Gives Insight into the Biology of Mental Disorders," *The Oregonian.* Dec. 31, 1992, page C4.

BIBLIOGRAPHY (continued)

Mainstream Inc., 3 Bethesda Metro Center, Suite #830, Bethesda, MD 20814. (301) 654-2400 (v/tdd), (301) 654-2403 (fax). Bi-monthly newsletter, *In the Mainstream* contains up-to-date ADA information. $20 per year. Mainstream also has an information packet of 11 articles on the accommodation process with examples of successful accommodations for $20.

Mancuso, L. L. ''Reasonable Accommodations for Workers with Psychiatric Disabilities,'' *Psychosocial Rehabilitation Journal,* 14, 3–19, 1990.

New Jersey Bell. *New Horizons: A Guide for Supervisors Working with the Handicapped* (pamphlet for Jersey Bell employees, but includes general information as well), 1984.

New York Telephone. *Supervisor Responsibilities Toward Handicapped Individuals, Special Disabled Veterans and Vietnam Veterans* (pamphlet for New York Telephone employees, but includes general information as well), 1983.

President's Committee on Employment of People with Disabilities. *Ready, Willing, and Available: A Business Guide for Hiring People with Disabilities.* Revised August 1992. (202) 376-6200 (voice), (202) 376-6205 (TDD), (202) 376-6219 (fax). The President's Committee also has pamphlets on working with people with specific disabilities.

Public Attitudes Toward People with Disabilities. Available for $25 from National Organization on Disability, 910 16th Street NW, Suite 600, Washington, DC 20006.

U.S. Department of Labor. *An Employer's Guide to Dealing with Substance Abuse,* published in October 1990. Brochure available from the National Clearinghouse for Alcohol and Drug Information, P.O. Box 2345, Rockville, MD 20852, (301) 468-2600 or (800) 729-6686.

NOTES

FOR OTHER FIFTY-MINUTE SELF-STUDY BOOKS
SEE THE BACK OF THIS BOOK.

NOTES

FOR OTHER FIFTY-MINUTE SELF-STUDY BOOKS
SEE THE BACK OF THIS BOOK.

Management Training (continued):

	Title	No.
V	Team Building—Revised	118-X
	Training Managers to Train	43-2
	Training Methods That Work	082-5
	Understanding Organizational Change	71-8
V	Working Together in a Multicultural Organization	85-8

Personal Improvement:

	Title	No.
V	Attitude: Your Most Priceless Possession—Revised	011-6
	Business Etiquette & Professionalism	32-9
	Concentration!	073-6
	The Continuously Improving Self: A Personal Guide to TQM	151-1
V	Developing Positive Assertiveness	38-6
	Developing Self-Esteem	66-1
	Finding Your Purpose: A Guide to Personal Fulfillment	072-8
	From Technical Specialist to Supervisor	194-X
	Managing Anger	114-7
	Memory Skills in Business	56-4
	Organizing Your Workspace	125-2
V	Personal Time Management	22-X
	Plan Your Work—Work Your Plan!	078-7
	Self-Empowerment	128-7
	Stop Procrastinating: Get to Work!	88-2
	Successful Self-Management	26-2
	The Telephone & Time Management	53-X
	Twelve Steps to Self-Improvement	102-3

Human Resources & Wellness:

	Title	No.
	Attacking Absenteeism	042-6
V	Balancing Home & Career—Revised	35-3
	Downsizing Without Disaster	081-7
	Effective Performance Appraisals—Revised	11-4
	Effective Recruiting Strategies	127-9
	Employee Benefits with Cost Control	133-3
	Giving & Receiving Criticism	023-X
	Guide to Affirmative Action	54-8
	Guide to OSHA	180-5
	Health Strategies for Working Women	079-5
V	High Performance Hiring	088-4
V	Job Performance & Chemical Dependency	27-0
V	Managing Personal Change	74-2
	Managing Upward: Managing Your Boss	131-7
V	Men and Women: Partners at Work	009-4
V	Mental Fitness: A Guide to Stress Management	15-7
	New Employee Orientation	46-7
	Office Management: A Guide to Productivity	005-1
	Overcoming Anxiety	29-9
	Personal Counseling	14-9
	Personal Wellness: Achieving Balance for Healthy Living	21-3
	Preventing Job Burnout	23-8

Human Resources & Wellness (continued):

	Title	No.
	Productivity at the Workstation: Wellness & Fitness at Your Desk	41-8
	Professional Excellence for Secretaries	52-1
	Quality Interviewing—Revised	13-0
	Sexual Harassment in the Workplace	153-8
	Stress That Motivates: Self-Talk Secrets for Success	150-3
	Wellness in the Workplace	20-5
	Winning at Human Relations	86-6
	Writing a Human Resources Manual	70-X
V	Your First Thirty Days in a New Job	003-5

Communications & Creativity:

	Title	No.
	The Art of Communicating	45-9
V	Writing Business Proposals & Reports—Revised	25-4
V	The Business of Listening	34-3
	Business Report Writing	122-8
	Creative Decision Making	098-1
V	Creativity in Business	67-X
	Dealing Effectively with the Media	116-3
V	Effective Presentation Skills	24-6
	Facilitation Skills	199-6
	Fifty One-Minute Tips to Better Communication	071-X
	Formatting Letters & Memos on the Microcomputer	130-9
	Influencing Others	84-X
V	Making Humor Work	61-0
	Speedreading in Business	78-5
	Technical Presentation Skills	55-6
	Technical Writing in the Corporate World	004-3
	Think on Your Feet	117-1
	Visual Aids in Business	77-7
	Writing Fitness	35-1

Customer Service/Sales Training:

	Title	No.
	Beyond Customer Service: The Art of Customer Retention	115-5
V	Calming Upset Customers	65-3
V	Customer Satisfaction—Revised	084-1
	Effective Sales Management	31-0
	Exhibiting at Tradeshows	137-6
	Improving Your Company Image	136-8
	Managing Quality Customer Service	83-1
	Measuring Customer Satisfaction	178-3
	Professional Selling	42-4
V	Quality Customer Service—Revised	95-5
	Restaurant Server's Guide—Revised	08-4
	Sales Training Basics—Revised	119-8
	Telemarketing Basics	60-2
V	Telephone Courtesy & Customer Service—Revised	064-7

Small Business & Financial Planning:

The Accounting Cycle	146-5
The Basics of Budgeting	134-1
Consulting for Success	006-X
Creative Fund Raising	181-3
Credits & Collections	080-9
Direct Mail Magic	075-2
Financial Analysis: Beyond the Basics	132-5
Financial Planning with Employee Benefits	90-4
Marketing Your Consulting or Professional Services	40-8
Personal Financial Fitness—Revised	89-0
Publicity Power	82-3
Starting Your New Business—Revised	144-9
Understanding Financial Statements	22-1
Writing & Implementing a Marketing Plan	083-3

Adult Literacy & Learning:

Adult Learning Skills	175-9
Basic Business Math	24-8
Becoming an Effective Tutor	28-0
Building Blocks of Business Writing	095-7
Clear Writing	094-9
The College Experience: Your First Thirty Days on Campus	07-8
Easy English	198-8
Going Back to School: An Adult Perspective	142-2
Introduction to Microcomputers: The Least You Should Know	087-6
Language, Customs & Protocol for Foreign Students	097-3
Improve Your Reading	086-8
Returning to Learning: Getting Your G.E.D.	02-7
Study Skills Strategies—Revised	05-X
Vocabulary Improvement	124-4

Career/Retirement & Life Planning:

Career Discovery—Revised	07-6
Developing Strategic Resumes	129-5
Effective Networking	30-2
I Got the Job!—Revised	121-X
Job Search That Works	105-8
Plan B: Protecting Your Career from Change	48-3
Preparing for Your Interview	33-7